HABITUDES®

IMAGES
THAT FORM
LEADERSHIP
HABITS &
ATTITUDES

BY

DR TIM
ELMORE

My special thanks to Keith Drury, who inspired many of the images you'll find in this series of books. Keith was the first person who taught me leadership truths through the power of pictures. Thanks, Keith, for being such a good mentor.

Published in Atlanta, Georgia by "Growing Leaders, Inc." (www.GrowingLeaders.com)

ISBN: 0-9792940-2-9
Printed in the United States of America
Library of Congress Cataloguing-in-Publication Data

TABLE OF CONTENTS

A WORD ABOUT IMAGES

We live in a culture rich with images. We grew up with photographs, TV, movies, video, MTV and DVDs. Now YouTube and smart phones make it possible to view videos almost anytime or anywhere. We can't escape the power of the visual image - and most of us don't want to.

I've learned over my career that most of us are visual learners. We like to see a picture, not just hear a word. Author Leonard Sweet says that images are the language of the 21st century, not words. Some of the best communicators in history taught using the power of the metaphor and image. One example is Martin Luther King, Jr. and his "I Have a Dream" speech during the Civil Rights movement. Tom Peters once wrote, "The best leaders... almost without exception and at every level, are master users of stories and symbols."

Why? Because pictures stick. We remember pictures long after words have left us. When we hear a speech, we often remember the stories from that speech more than the phrases used by the speaker, because they painted a picture inside of us. Pictures communicate far more than mere words. In fact, words are helpful only as they conjure up a picture in our minds. Most of us think in pictures. If I say the word "elephant" to you, you don't picture the letters: e-l-e-p-h-a-n-t. You picture a big gray animal. Pictures are what we file away in our minds. They enable us to store huge volumes of information. There's an old phrase that has stood the test of time: A picture is worth a thousand words. I believe it's true. I pursued a degree in both commercial art as well as theology in college. That's when I recognized the power of the image. Now I get to combine the power of teaching leadership principles with the power of pictures. I hope they linger in your mind and heart. I hope you discover layers of reality in them as you grow. I trust they'll impact you as profoundly as they have me.

This book is part of a series, designed to furnish pictures you can discuss with a community of people. I encourage you to go through the series in a group. Each picture contains layers of reality, and your discussion can go as deep as you allow it to go. The books are created to guide you on your leadership journey. They are based on the fact that leadership isn't merely one-dimensional. It runs 360 degrees. We influence others all around us. We must first lead ourselves. Then, we will also influence those above us. Next, we will influence those around us. Finally, we influence those for whom we are responsible. This book covers the art of leading others. Once I lead myself well, others should be magnetically attracted to follow. Next, I learn to connect with others. At this point, I become their friend. Finally, when I learn to take others to a place they want to go—I become their leader. Through the power of images, this book will enable you to discuss principles that will make you a better leader for others to follow.

Some sociologists describe this generation as EPIC: Experiential, Participatory, Image-driven and Connected. If that's true, I believe we'll get the most out of resources that give us an image, an experience and a way to connect with each other. Each of these books provides you not only with an image, but a handful of discussion questions, a self-assessment and an exercise in which you can participate. Dive in and experience each one of them. My hope is that they become signposts that guide you, and warn you, and inform you on your leadership journey.

Dr. Tim Elmore

The Mirror Effect

AS A LEADER, YOUR FOLLOWERS WILL BE A REFLECTION OF YOU. NOT ONLY WILL YOU ATTRACT OTHERS LIKE YOURSELF, BUT OVER TIME, THOSE WHO FOLLOW YOU WILL MIRROR BOTH YOUR NEGATIVE AND POSITIVE CHARACTERISTICS.

Since the beginning of time, humans have been preoccupied with their looks. Consequently, we've searched for ways to see our reflections and seek out available mirrors. The still water of a clear pool, in fact, was man's first mirror.

With the rise of the Bronze Age, in about 3,500 B.C., polished metal had become the favored material among Sumerians in Mesopotamia, as well as Egyptians and Hebrews. By 328 B.C., the Greeks had established a school for mirror craftsmanship, and by the rise of the Roman Empire, manufacturing mirrors had become a flourishing business. Eventually, gold mirrors were the craze. In fact, head servants would even demand personalized gold mirrors to be allotted in place of their wages!

The first glass mirrors allowed for a far more precise reflection. They debuted in Venice, Italy, in 1300, under the hands of Venetian glass blowers. By 1687, Frenchman Bernard Perrot had patented a method for rolling out smooth, undistorted sheets of glass, resulting in the hand-held and full-length mirrors we know today. At last, man had fashioned an instrument that offered a perfect reflection of himself. Mirrors remain an important part of most any dorm, bath, or bedroom in modern day culture.

The mirror reminds us of a helpful leadership principle. Leaders, in fact, have their own unique mirror—their followers. I call this the mirror effect. Within 18 to 24 months, leaders will find that they cannot blame someone else for the atmosphere and attitude of the organization. They are the reason for that atmosphere. By design, or by default, the leader has set the tone. While the speed at which they do this will vary, any leader's example will eventually impact the entire team. Once this happens, the followers become a mirror, reflecting the good or bad values and virtues of the leader. As Rick Warren describes it, "If you want to know the temperature of an organization, put a thermometer in the leader's mouth."

For years, I worked with college students in San Diego and oversaw our intern program. We had dozens of interns serving, and at the end of every year, it became somewhat predictable for me to hear people say:

"Hey, Tim, your intern sounds just like you."

"I could see you in them."

"I could tell they have been around you, Tim."

My explanation is simple. It's the mirror effect. While each intern retained their own personality, they couldn't help but reflect the style, values and even flaws of their leader. Dr. John Maxwell further illustrates this with the Law of Magnetism: Leaders attract who they "are," not who they "want." In other words, like attracts like. But there's another law at work here beyond Magnetism. Call it the Law of Emulation. Leaders must model the life they want their followers to live because people will emulate them. In a nutshell, the top rule of management is: people do what people see.

Over the years, I've enjoyed asking this question to audiences at leadership conferences on university campuses, or with corporations: What virtues do you wish your people possessed? On a pad of paper, I jot down the responses: "I wish they were more committed... had a better attitude... possessed more passion... were more friendly..." and the list goes on. Then I take the list and ask, "Do you have these qualities? Do you model these virtues?"

People do what people see. They are mirrors.

The Mirror Effect underscores a principle that leaders must never forget—the power of example. You can talk all you want about behaviors and expectations for your organization, but ultimately, the life you model will be the lecture that gets through. Dr. Albert Schweitzer once said, "Example is not the most important thing about leadership. It is the only thing." Ask any manager. Ask any teacher. In fact, ask any parent. Kids do what kids see.

Recently, I was in the home of a neighbor who was teaching his son the virtue of honesty and integrity. He was so proud of their discussions over the past month. My friend was convinced he was getting through. As we were talking, however, the phone rang. As his son ran to grab it, my neighbor yelled, "If it's for me, tell them I'm not here!"

Hmmm. Now what do you suppose that young boy concludes about honesty? "Dad's lectures say we should be honest at all times, but I guess it's just talk. When honesty becomes inconvenient, we don't have to actually practice it." Chances are, this boy will grow up believing honesty is important to talk about, but when it becomes inconvenient, who cares?

"Paying the Piper" is an old black and white movie about a father's challenges in raising his teenage daughter. In one of the scenes, the girl asks permission to attend the high school dance with an older boy.

Reluctantly, the dad allows her to go, though he remains protective. He doesn't want anything in the "real world" to harm his little girl. Waiting up for her on the night of the dance, the father is faced with his worst nightmare when the police show up at his front door. They inform him that his daughter and her date had been drinking and carelessly drove off of a bridge. Both died instantly.

The father is in anguish. "How could any restaurant, bar, or liquor store sell alcohol to a minor?" He determines to find the culprit, and he spends endless time and money investigating the crime, but to no avail. He failed in his search. In one final scene, he slumps in his living room chair. He is weary. He decides a drink would help his tired nerves at this point. But opening his liquor cabinet, he's stunned to find his bottle missing, replaced by a note that said, "Dear Dad, I know you like your Scotch to help you celebrate. I thought you wouldn't mind sharing it with me."

People do what people see—at home, at work, at school, wherever there is a leader. This explains why the followers of Martin Luther King Jr. acted so differently from the followers of Malcolm X. It explains why the Nazi regime, under Adolf Hitler, was so violent, and why the followers of Mahatma Gandhi were so peaceful. Just look at the leader. It's the mirror effect.

REFLECT AND RESPOND

Leaders create the atmosphere and attitudes of their organizations. By design or default, they set the tone for their entire team. Why do you think example is more powerful than mere words?

_____

_____

_____

As leaders, we must realize the "mirror effect" is constantly at work. Think of a leader that you know and respect. List several ways that the mirror effect is always at work in his or her life.

_____

_____

_____

SELF-ASSESSMENT

Take an honest look at your own life. More than likely, there are aspects that involve following people as well as leading people. Consider these questions and how the mirror effect might be at work in each one:

Who am I mirroring?

_____

_____

_____

Who might be mirroring, or reflecting, me?

_____

_____

_____

What positive qualities do I possess? How might others be emulating these qualities?

_____

_____

_____

What negative qualities do I possess? How might others be emulating these qualities?

_____

_____

_____

EXERCISE

Take some time to "people watch." This week, observe different groups of people and how the mirror effect is at work. What similarities, or differences, can you pinpoint among the girls and guys? Does anyone conspicuously stand out as a leader? Discuss why.

_____

_____

_____

As a leader, do you wish your team possessed different attitudes, or virtues? What might this say about you?

_____

_____

_____

Rivers and Floods

FLOODS AND RIVERS ARE BOTH BODIES OF WATER. FLOODS DAMAGE. RIVERS
ARE USEFUL IN MANY WAYS. THE DIFFERENCE? FOCUS. LEADERS MUST CHANNEL
PEOPLE, TIME AND MONEY TOWARD ONE FOCUSED VISION.

I have a picture indelibly etched in my memory. When I was a kid, I remember a
horrifying flood sweeping through a town not far from where we lived. I watched
the TV intently as reporters showed the expanding body of murky water run
through streets, over yards and into houses, restaurants and stores. The rushing
water seemed to demolish everything in its path. In my mind, I can still see people
standing on the tops of their cars weeping, as they watched their homes collapse
and float away—piece by piece.

What started as a simple rainstorm ended up filling the nearby rivers and eventually
flowing unmercifully into neighborhoods and strip malls. I remember thinking:
How can such a simple thing as water do such damage? Some of my friends took
a while to recover from the flood. One of them, in fact, wanted nothing to do with
water for over a year. For him, a large body of water without some boundary was
a frightening thing.

This is a picture of an important leadership principle. Many organizations begin
very focused, like a river. The leaders possess an idea they want to implement.
Soon, however, in their zeal to grow, they begin expanding far beyond the
boundaries of their initial vision. If they are good at making widgets, they reason,
why not make other products as well? Before long, in the name of meeting needs,
generating revenue, or just plain growth—they become a flood instead of a river.
They lose all focus and sprawl out in every direction. Like a flood, they end up
damaging things. Floods can be shallow, unrestrained, muddy and harmful.

Far too many organizations become floods. Take IBM for instance. In the
beginning, when IBM focused on mainframe computers, the company made a ton
of money. By the 1980s, however, IBM expanded their product line and barely
broke even. In 1991, they were making more products than ever, yet, the company
wound up losing $2.8 billion. That's almost $8 million a day!

It's interesting. This rule of leadership is counter intuitive. It works the opposite of what we might think. It seems logical that enlarging product lines would always mean greater profit. It's actually the other way around. Staying focused on your central vision and strength is the key to growth. The airline industry is a good example. "People Express" launched as an airline that focused on no frills, low cost flights. At the first taste of success, they decided to expand beyond that vision. They began to provide first class seats, food, etc. Their profits dropped. In fact, they went out of business.

In contrast, Southwest Airlines entered the industry with a clear, focused vision, similar to People Express. Yet, they stuck to their strengths, and for years they've been a rare, profitable company in the airline business. Southwest Airlines refused to diversify; they remained a river. Rivers are much more narrow than floods. They move in one direction. They are a source for both electricity and transportation. Why? Vision and focus. Leaders must own a focused vision, or the organization will spill-out in too many directions. If the leader isn't focused, the team will chase after every new idea. They will fall prey to every vendor wanting to capitalize on the success. Clear and focused vision harnesses energy. Just watch your team for a while. People lose energy when their direction in life is fuzzy. But they get energized when they catch a clear vision.

Just over fifty years ago, Walt Disney gathered his inner-circle to share his idea of building "Disneyland." It would be known as the "happiest place on earth." Walt's vision was clear and focused. As his team began to get excited about the vision, however, one of the members asked, "Who are you gonna get to build it?" Confidently, Walt responded, "I know exactly who I want to build it. Find me the man who helped put the U.S. Navy back in the Pacific after the bombing of Pearl Harbor. I figure he can do it."

It didn't take long for Walt's team to identify this man. His name was Joe Fowler. Admiral Joe Fowler. Retired Admiral Joe Fowler. When Disney showed up at Fowler's door and challenged him to build a theme park, Joe laughed. "You don't understand. I'm retired. I'm through." Disney quickly realized this guy was going to require some work. Placing pictures on the wall, Walt began to storyboard. Describing in great detail the feel, look, smell, sound and even taste of the park—Joe bought in. He stepped out of retirement and oversaw Disneyland's construction.

Twenty years later, the idea of Disney World was proposed—and can you guess who was hired to supervise the project? Joe Fowler. This time he was 77 years old. When the Disney team approached him a second time, he sighed again, "You don't understand. I'm retired. I'm through." But as pictures were posted and the vision was cast for their biggest project yet, Joe couldn't help but buy in. He ditched retirement again and oversaw the building of Disney World.

The story goes on. Ten years later, EPCOT was built in Orlando. Disney once again looked to Joe Fowler to lead the construction. He was now 87 years old.

Joe repeated his objection: "You don't understand. I'm retired. I'm through." But Disney knew Joe was the man. His team communicated the clear, focused vision again. Joe lit up, stepped out of retirement and oversaw the project.

What a picture of the energy that accompanies clear vision. Joe's favorite phrase, "I'm retired. I'm through," was changed to, "You don't have to die 'til you want to." Hmmm. I often wonder how much energy remains bottled up in people because they never learn to focus, or they just plain fail to tap into a clear vision.

Here is the irony of this principle. My friend Mike Kendrick explained it with the following phrase: What you focus on expands. Read that sentence again. Now think about it. If I tell you to focus on finding Toyota Camrys on the road, you will notice these cars everywhere. Why? Because what you focus on expands. So, the goal of a leader is to focus, not expand. Growth is a product of focus. Clarify the vision. Focus your people, time, energy and resources. Remember this: just because you CAN do something doesn't mean you SHOULD. Intensify. Don't diversify.

In order to accomplish this focus, it's important to zero in on a handful of words. In fact, maybe just one word (or concept) that becomes your own. It describes your identity and vision. Some of the best selling products on the market "own" such words. Crest toothpaste owns the word "cavities." FedEx owns the word "overnight." Volvo owns the words "automobile safety." As they focus their energies on a single concept, these companies go deeper and expand in one area. They are like a river, moving in one direction. And being a river is about clear vision and a sharp focus.

REFLECT AND RESPOND

Many organizations begin very focused, like a river, but as they expand they lose their initial vision and become a flood. Using the examples that were given in this chapter, what are some of the benefits of a clear, focused vision?

_____

_____

_____

_____

Try to think of organizations—either historical or current—who lost their vision. List them below with a brief explanation of how you believe they lost their vision. What was the end result?

_____

_____

_____

_____

The water in a river represents the people, time, energy and resources invested in your organization. So if you're going to be a river, you've got to channel your water well. Consider these questions.

How many activities are you trying to perform? How about your organization? How thin have you spread yourself? Are you more like a flood or a river?

_____

_____

_____

What should you cut out of your life or trim back, in order to be more productive?

_____

_____

_____

Here's the challenge. Ask yourself: What word do we own? Ask outsiders what word comes to mind when they think of your organization?

_____

_____

_____

Exercise

Consider an organization you're involved with and discuss within your team the "word" that most clearly describes your vision. What's your focus? Do you think your customers would agree?

_____

_____

_____

_____

Just for fun, clump your group together and tie a rope around them. Lead the group outside and see if they can stay together. Do they listen to you? Does each person try to go their own direction, or do they focus on working together?

_____

_____

_____

_____

The Paul Revere Principle

PAUL REVERE AND WILLIAM DAWES BOTH MADE A MIDNIGHT RIDE, BUT ONLY ONE WAS ABLE TO CONNECT WITH AND INFLUENCE PEOPLE. THE TEST OF A LEADER'S CREDIBILITY LIES IN HIS OR HER ABILITY TO MOBILIZE OTHERS.

Just outside of Boston on April 18th, 1775, a young stable boy overheard two British soldiers talking. They hinted of an attack on the colonists in New England, and they said something about the townsmen having "hell to pay" tomorrow. The young boy ran to inform a silversmith by the name of Paul Revere. After careful thought, Revere determined to mobilize the area against the attack the British were planning. And the rest, as they say, is history.

Paul Revere made his famous "midnight ride," which actually began about 10:00 p.m. that night. He raced on horseback through the towns and villages surrounding Boston, challenging locals to get up and defend their country! By the next morning, as the Redcoats secretly made their way inland, they were met in Lexington by a huge group of volunteers, American patriots. They were shocked, to say the least. The British were unprepared and outdone that morning—and the Revolutionary War was underway.

An interesting bit of trivia from this story is that Paul Revere wasn't the only Patriot to make a midnight ride. A tanner by the name of William Dawes also took the ride. He rode on a similar horse, covered a similar amount of territory and carried an identical message, but Dawes had difficulty getting anyone to act. In fact, he was so poor at mobilizing folks, historians assumed for years Dawes must have traveled to pro-British towns. But, alas, he hadn't. He simply lacked the capability to mobilize people, even for a cause they agreed with.

This contrast illustrates another important leadership principle. I call it the "Paul Revere Principle." When you boil down the essence of leadership to its bare minimum, it's about mobilizing others to act. Paul Revere was able to connect with and influence townspeople to get up and respond. William Dawes, on the other hand, couldn't get a man to turn over in bed!

(Well—that may be a bit of an exaggeration.) For some reason, though, Dawes lacked the credibility, communication skills, aptitude, trust and respect to move people toward taking a risk.

So what is it, then, that enables a leader to motivate people to action? There are many answers to that question, but let me suggest a few:

1. INSIGHT – PEOPLE LISTEN TO YOU BECAUSE OF WHAT YOU KNOW.
   Example: Ben Franklin. Ben influenced people through his knowledge, wisdom and insight.

2. RELATIONSHIPS – PEOPLE LISTEN BECAUSE OF WHO YOU KNOW.
   Example: Oprah Winfrey. Although she has several influential qualities, she is very well connected and both colleagues and TV viewers like her.

3. SACRIFICE – PEOPLE LISTEN BECAUSE OF WHAT YOU'VE SUFFERED.
   Example: Mother Teresa. Harvard grads and U.S. presidents listened because of her sacrificial life.

4. ABILITIES – PEOPLE LISTEN BECAUSE OF WHAT YOU ARE ABLE TO DO.
   Example: Michael Jordan. His credibility came from his unmatched skills on the basketball court.

5. EXPERIENCE – PEOPLE LISTEN BECAUSE OF WHAT YOU'VE ACHIEVED.
   Example: Colin Powell or Norman Schwarzkopf. Their credibility came from their military success.

6. INTUITION – PEOPLE LISTEN BECAUSE OF WHAT YOU SENSE.
   Example: Thomas Edison or Steve Jobs. They saw a new world coming before the rest of us did.

7. CHARACTER – PEOPLE LISTEN BECAUSE OF YOUR INTEGRITY.
   Example: Billy Graham. His sermons aren't flashy, but he's a man of his word. He walks the talk.

8. HUMILITY – PEOPLE LISTEN BECAUSE OF YOUR HEART.
   Example: Dan Cathy. The president of Chick-fil-A by serving his employees and customers.

9. RELEVANCE – PEOPLE LISTEN BECAUSE YOU IDENTIFY WITH THEIR NEEDS.
   Example: Martin Luther King, Jr. He identified with common folks; he marched and bled with them.

10. CONVICTIONS – PEOPLE LISTEN BECAUSE OF YOUR PASSION.
    Example: Winston Churchill. His passion and conviction stirred the Allies to fight until they won.

Let me ask you a question: Why do people listen to you? What reasons do you give them to follow you? Good leaders find a way to connect with people. They earn their right to be followed. They build bridges of relationship that can bear the weight of principle.

Since 1983, I have been mentored by and worked with Dr. John Maxwell. He told me a great story that I think really illustrates this principle. Early in his career, he became the new senior minister at a church, and because he was replacing the founding minister, Orval Butcher, John found a number of charter members who loved "the old" and despised "the new." He had replaced their hero. One such man was Harry Mitchell. Harry wouldn't have anything to do with John. He didn't respond to John's attempts to befriend him and would gripe about any change that John made. Finally, he asked Harry's wife what the problem was. She confided in him that Harry loved his former leader and since John replaced this leader, Harry couldn't like him. It was at this point John took action. He called Harry and asked if they could meet, to which Harry reluctantly agreed. After some small talk, John leaned forward and said, "I have a question for you, Harry. Would you mind taking a minute and telling me about Reverend Butcher?" Harry lit up like a light. Immediately, he began telling stories about how Reverend Butcher had married and buried family and friends, and how he'd helped him in many tough times. He went on for several minutes. When Harry finished, John leaned forward and responded, "Harry, I have to tell you—I agree. Reverend Butcher was, and is, a great leader. And I think you should continue loving him just the way you do today. He deserves all that love." This was not only liberating for Harry, but it was disarming, too. John paused and continued, "Now, I have another question for you. After you love Reverend Butcher with all that love, if there's any love left over, could I have it?"

Harry's heart began to break. He knew exactly what was happening. His new leader would let him go on with his emotional tie to his former leader and was simply asking for "the leftovers." Harry was speechless. Both of the men just sat there and wept. Harry eventually got up and for the first time, initiated a hug with his new leader. It was a breakthrough. Following that day, I got to watch Harry support John and connect with him like never before. In fact, Harry would often linger on Sunday mornings and once everyone was gone, he'd sneak up on Dr. Maxwell and give him a huge bear hug, whispering, "This is the love I got left over."

REFLECT AND RESPOND

Everyone must earn the right to be followed. This chapter opened with the example of Paul Revere's ability to connect with and influence the townspeople to action. After his story, I list ten reasons that enable leaders to motivate their people to action. Reflect on why people follow you. Which reasons are true about your influence with people? Why do people follow you?

_____

_____

_____

As leaders, the question of influence isn't about the "what," but the "how." The way we treat our team members is an important piece of the puzzle in motivating them to action. How might this consideration affect your influence?

_____

_____

_____

SELF-ASSESSMENT

Earlier, I told the story of how John Maxwell connected with Harry Mitchell. I believe John practiced four roles in that relationship. Evaluate yourself on these roles. Why did you score yourself this way?

A HOST: Do you initiate contact with people so they are comfortable? You're a host, not a guest.

< POOR 1　2　3　4　5　6　7　8　9　10 EXCELLENT >

A DOCTOR: Do you poke and prod with questions, so the focus is on them and not on you?

< POOR 1　2　3　4　5　6　7　8　9　10 EXCELLENT >

A COUNSELOR: Do you actively listen after posing a question, allowing the person to see your desire to understand, and not just speak?

< POOR 1　2　3　4　5　6　7　8　9　10 EXCELLENT >

A TOUR GUIDE: Do you earn the right to lead people to a destination that is possibly unreachable without you?

< POOR 1　2　3　4　5　6　7　8　9　10 EXCELLENT >

EXERCISE

Prepare a survey and with a group, take it to a park, mall, or some public setting. How many people can you get to take your survey? Do different people in your group get different responses? Did one person have unusual success, or another more difficulty? Why might some be able to motivate others easily, while others struggle? Talk about what happened with your group.

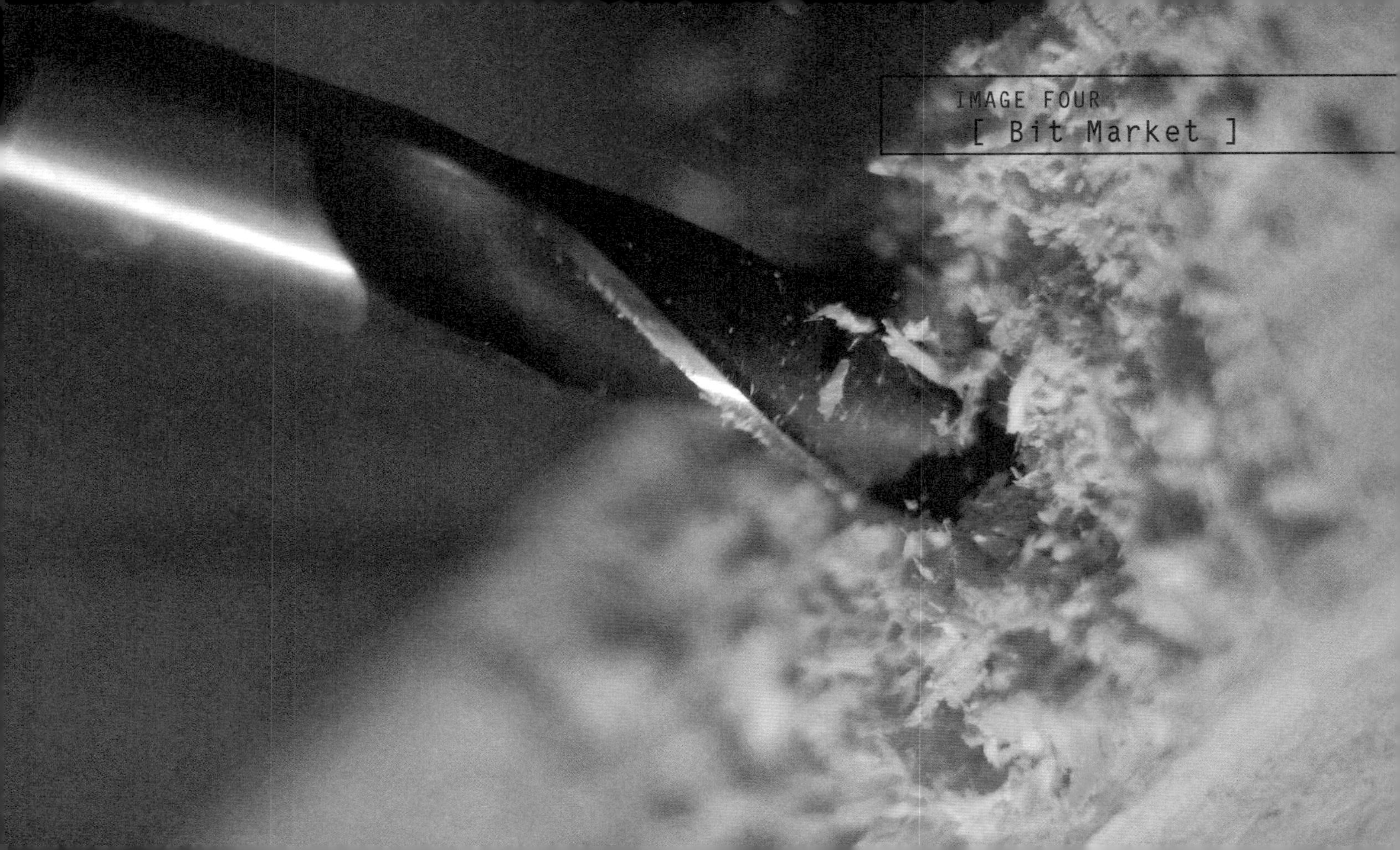

IMAGE FOUR
[Bit Market]

Bit Market

A DRILL COMPANY LEARNED: THERE'S NO MARKET FOR DRILL BITS—ONLY HOLES. GOOD LEADERS DON'T CONFUSE METHODS WITH THEIR MISSION. THEY SELL RESULTS, NOT PROGRAMS. THEY KEEP THEIR EYES ON THE BIG PICTURE.

A drill company hired a new president to lead them. They were excited about the future and wanted the president to see how much influence they already had in the marketplace. On his first day, department managers gave speeches on their company's control over the bit market. Selling 60% of all drill bits purchased in America, they couldn't help but be proud of their status.

That afternoon, the president stood up and responded. After thanking them for their speeches, he confronted them with a harsh reality. "While I'm excited about our drill bit sales, we must remember one fact: there is no market for drill bits." He paused and smiled. "The market is for holes." Those employees discovered an important principle that day. This company had focused so intently on their product—their method for making a hole—they forgot it was only the means to an end. People buy drill bits to make a hole. And the moment someone comes up with a better way to make a hole, the drill bit becomes obsolete.

Effective leaders help their team see the big picture perspective. They never lose sight of the intended result. Because of this, they are open to new ideas, methods and innovations toward reaching their goal. For instance, the next best way to make a hole in a piece of wood might be a laser gun, requiring no drill bits at all. This new method would require a whole new skill set, technology, and even new team members! Hmmm—it's enough to humble any leader. Bottom line: our world changes too fast to ever "marry a method."

One of the easiest traps that entangle leaders is falling in love with a method or program. When that happens, leaders become blinded to new ways of reaching their goal. Sometimes, our egos cloud our thinking. Someone once said that if the railroad industry had realized they were really in the transportation business, they would have been the first people in the airline industry. Take a minute to reflect. How many organizations have failed because they focused on their "drill bit?"

Hundreds of companies across America who once led their industries have either fallen behind or have fallen completely out of business. Why? They saw only their drill bit—and forgot the hole.

Companies that see the big picture, on the other hand, are open to change and stay relevant. For example, H&R Block began years ago because they wanted to help people with their finances. The company started as a bookkeeping service for small corporations who couldn't afford a full-time bookkeeper. In order to attract business, they offered a free tax service and within a short time, they made a huge discovery. Customers would sign up for their bookkeeping service, just to get their taxes handled. In other words, H&R Block recognized what their customers really wanted and adjusted their methods to meet that need. Today, H&R Block is known as a tax service. In fact, they handle the tax forms of more Americans than any other company in their industry.

Take the game of football. Up until 1906, college football was a low-scoring, slow running game. That year, the forward pass was legalized. It represented a whole new way to move the ball downfield. That season, however, everyone ignored this new rule and continued to focus on what they already knew how to do. That is, everyone except for St. Louis University. They saw the potential of this change and created a whole new offense. The result? That season St. Louis outscored their opponents 402 to 11.

THE SIGMOID CURVE

So what allows a leader to be open to new ideas? What enables leaders to change when they need to? And just how does positive change take place in an organization today? The answer comes from a little diagram created by British educator, Charles Handy. It is called, The Sigmoid Curve. In several diagrams, Handy communicates how effective organizations experience growth and change.

HOW GROWTH HAPPENS

Notice the following diagram. It shows how a new organization grows. At first, the curve goes down, as time, money and people are invested. Eventually, they begin to grow, and the team enjoys success and even mastery of what they do. Over time, though, if they continue doing what they've always done, they will plateau. And if they refuse to change, the organization will experience decline. Sales, or interest, will drop. It's at this point most leaders make a change—Point B. The problem is, it's a little late. Momentum is gone and they're back in first gear. In other words, it feels like raising the dead to begin again.

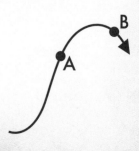

Changing Before You Have To

Charles Handy says a good leader will make the change much earlier, or at Point A. But if leaders do so, they will incur the wrath of many on their team. Why? Because nobody else sees the need for change. Everything seems fine. So, for a time, the leader will appear wrong. From the time he makes the change (Point A), to the time everyone recognizes the wisdom behind his decision (Point B), the organization experiences a "Period of Chaos." The team feels like it's in a state of flux, and no one knows what they are doing.

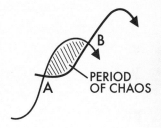

Chaos is Our Constant Companion

The good news is—this period ends well. Eventually, the team sees that the leader made an early move to stay on top of the game. Consequently, the leader earns the team's trust. The more challenging news is that the organization must begin a new Sigmoid Curve. They can enjoy their new idea for a season, but must stay open for the next change. In fact, good leaders are continually improving their organizations and making positive changes. This means that chaos might just be a constant companion for those team members. But this is good! Everyone is forced to keep their eyes on the mission, not the method.

Effective leaders welcome change. They sell holes (goals) to their stakeholders, not drill bits (programs). In fact, they're constantly looking for new ways to make holes. They keep their eyes on the dream, not the drill bit. Finally, any "one" method doesn't bind them. And the reason is simple. Good leaders pursue results.

Reflect and Respond

Effective leaders help their team see the big picture. Because they never lose sight of the intended result, successful leaders are open to new ideas to reach their goal. As you reflect on this *Habitude*, what "hole" are you trying to drill... at work? In your family? At school?

_____

_____

_____

Choose one of the above areas. What is one new way to drill this hole? In other words, what new idea might more effectively reach your goal in that area?

_____

_____

_____

_____

Sometimes leaders focus on "pet" issues, while forgetting the bigger picture. What can you do to keep from falling into this same trap? What prevents you from trying new ideas?

_____

_____

_____

_____

Self-Assessment

As leaders, we tend to have "pet programs," or favorite ideas. These can be "drill bits" that blind us from more effective ways of reaching our goal—better ways to drill our hole. Evaluate what hinders you:

1. My pride & ego:
   If I create a program, it's difficult for me to see the value of other ideas: Yes / No

2. My perspective:
   It is often difficult for me to see an issue from more than one angle: Yes / No

3. My insecurities:
   I can get defensive, or competitive, if I'm committed to an idea: Yes / No

Exercise

Bring a bag of oddly shaped objects, tools or utensils to a team meeting. Have each team member pick one and imagine several new uses for the item. See the objects with new eyes. Brainstorm what they could do.

Next, think about new ways to achieve your goals as a team. Imagine new ways to drill a hole. List one way you could improve.

_____

_____

_____

_____

IMAGE FIVE

[Big Rocks First]

Big Rocks First

ROCKS ARE LIKE PRIORITIES. ONLY SO MANY ROCKS CAN FIT IN A JAR. ONLY SO MANY ACTIVITIES CAN FIT IN A WEEK. THE ISSUE ISN'T PRIORITIZING YOUR SCHEDULE, BUT SCHEDULING YOUR PRIORITIES. PUT IN THE BIG ROCKS FIRST.

A while back, I attended a seminar on time management. One morning, our speaker decided to give us a pop quiz. He pulled out a wide-mouth mason jar and set it on the table in front of him. Then he brought out several rocks—all shapes and sizes—and placed them arbitrarily into the jar. When no more rocks could fit, we noticed that much of his pile never made it into the jar. It was full. Afterward, he held it up and said, "This jar represents your typical week. The rocks represent the various activities in your week. When placed in randomly, everything simply won't fit in." Looking deep into our eyes he said, "Have you found this to be true?" Each of us nodded in agreement.

What he did next was fascinating. The speaker emptied out the jar he had filled, and began re-filling it with just the big rocks. He informed us that these rocks represented the "big priorities" in life: family, career, health, our studies, etc. Once the jar looked full, the man asked, "Is the jar full?" He received a unanimous, "Yes." "Really?" he asked. He then put the medium sized rocks in, which were just small enough to fit between the crevices of the big ones. Next, he reached under the table for a bucket of gravel. While shaking the jar, he dumped in the gravel, filling all the gaps. "Now is the jar full?" he asked. The speaker then pulled out a bucket of sand and began dumping it into the jar. It filled all remaining spaces between the rocks and the gravel. Finally, he grabbed a pitcher of water and poured it into the jar, until the jar was filled to the brim. "What's the principle of this illustration?" he asked the audience. "Cramming as much into one week as you possibly can!" was one response. "No," answered the speaker. "The point is, big rocks must go in first. When you put them in first, you'll find there's generally room for the smaller ones."

The same thing is true about day-to-day living. We fill our lives first with trivial things, only to find we don't have room for the most important things in life. This week, you probably have a full plate. As a student, you have tests, assignments, classes, e-mails and papers. As an employee, you have a job requiring even more things like meetings, calls and follow-ups. Or perhaps you're pulling double-duty, as both a student and an employee! How do you go about completing all of this? Some have no problem checking things off their to-do list, but others have difficulty just getting started! The real issue for either, though, falls in deciding where to start on your list.

When we have a to-do list, our human tendency is to start with the easier tasks. In fact, most people will do fun things, loud things, quick things, or easy things first. Usually, however, these are the less important tasks long-term—they're the small rocks. We must learn to do first things first. Another term for this Big Rock concept is the "Pareto Principle."

THE PARETO PRINCIPLE

Vilfredo Pareto was an Italian economist who made a discovery about a hundred years ago. He suggested that a principle is at work that applies to money, people and time. Some call it the 80/20 Principle. This principle teaches us about handling priorities. Here it is in a nutshell:

WHEN YOU PRACTICE THE RIGHT PRIORITIES, 20% OF YOUR EFFORT GETS YOU 80% OF YOUR DESIRED RESULTS.

For example, on a typical list of ten "to-do" items, two are often more significant in relation to the rest. In other words, 20% of the items are more productive than the other 80%. So why do we start with the less-important ones? Typically, it's because we can quickly cross them off our list and say, "Look at all the work I've done! See? I only have three things left to do!" The problem is, this plan doesn't necessarily translate into results. Activity does not equal accomplishment. The Pareto Principle teaches that focusing our attention on the most important activities, gains the highest return for our efforts. By focusing on the most important 20%, we accomplish 80% of our desired results. That means tackling items one and two on your list, especially if you can't fit them all in. First things first, not easy things first. Check out the diagram on the next page.

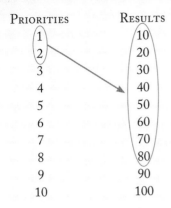

PRIORITIES   RESULTS

1	10
2	20
3	30
4	40
5	50
6	60
7	70
8	80
9	90
10	100

EXAMPLES OF THE 80/20 PRINCIPLE:

TIME—20% of your time produces 80% of the results.

WORK—20% of the people do 80% of the work.

GROWTH—20% of the programs furnish 80% of the growth.

FINANCES—20% of the people donate 80% of the money to charities.

LEADERSHIP—20% of the people make 80% of the decisions.

READING—20% of the book provides 80% of the helpful content.

LECTURES—20% of the class lecture offers 80% of the impact.

PICNICS—20% of the people eat 80% of the food. (Just kidding!)

Have you ever wished you had 30 hours in a day instead of 24? It sounds so nice, doesn't it? Six extra hours! We could get so much more done—spend more time with family, schedule more appointments, even catch up on sleep! But, do you really think adding more hours would solve our problems? Sure, we might cross off another "to-do," but we would likely add another at the same time! Putting more time in our day is not the solution to producing results. Our problem is, we don't handle our present schedules well. We get distracted, and even paralyzed, when so many items are screaming for our attention.

A lion tamer was once asked which "weapon" he would sacrifice first—his whip or his stool? He chose to keep the stool. This was puzzling until he explained why. The stool actually paralyzes the lion. When it is waved in front of him, the beast is unable to focus. The four separate legs create four separate focal points. The lion doesn't know which leg to focus on and because he can't decide, he can't attack. He's immobilized. Hmmm. Sound familiar?

The bottom line is simple. It's not about prioritizing our schedule—but rather, scheduling our priorities. We must choose the "big rocks" and place them first on our calendar.

REFLECT AND RESPOND

Our calendars reveal the hard evidence concerning the issue of scheduling priorities. What determines the items that fill your daily calendar? Why?

_____

_____

_____

_____

Do you tend to react more to the urgency of needs, or to the importance of needs? We live in constant tension between the urgent and the important. Are you allowing the urgent things to crowd out the important? Are your days filled by priorities, or by the relentless requests of others? How can you strike a balance between the urgent and the truly important?

_____

_____

_____

_____

SELF-ASSESSMENT

Your top priorities should revolve around the following three questions:

What is *required* of you? (What is a "must do"; what is absolutely necessary?)

_____

_____

_____

_____

What gives you the greatest *result*? (What will be the most productive?)

_____

_____

_____

_____

What is most *rewarding*? (What is most fulfilling when you do it?)

_____

_____

_____

_____

Pay attention to activities that show up in your answers. Those are your big rocks.

EXERCISE

On a separate sheet of paper, answer the following questions based on the 80/20 Principle. Look for places where your answers overlap. The answers that overlap will help you find your top 20% priorities as a leader.

1. Who defines the top 20% of influencers in whom you're investing your life?

2. What activities result in the greatest amount of results for your organization or team?

3. Who are the potential leaders you should train or equip for leadership?

4. When you lead, what gives you the deepest sense of fulfillment?

5. List other priorities you should pursue, based on your organization's mission.

The tragic story of Eastern Airline's 1972 crash into the Florida Everglades is a classic case of misplaced priorities. The now famous Flight 401 was bound from New York to Miami, with a heavy load of holiday passengers. As the plane approached the Miami airport, the pilot pushed the landing gear light. It didn't come on. Either the bulb was faulty, or the landing gear had not lowered. Over the next few minutes, as the plane circled the airport, everyone in the cockpit became preoccupied with the unlit bulb. Somehow, the plane's auto-pilot system disengaged and the plane began to descend, but due to the bulb distraction, no one noticed the lost altitude. Nor did the crew hear alarms warning of the plane's descent. Sadly, these highly paid pilots forgot the bigger picture and instead, got caught up in the seventy-five cent light bulb. They forgot the big rocks.

IMAGE SIX
[Duck Hunting]

IMAGE SIX
[Duck Hunting]

Duck Hunting

IN DUCK HUNTING, YOU DON'T HAVE TO GET ALL THE DUCKS TO HAVE A
SUCCESSFUL HUNT. LIKEWISE, LEADERS DON'T EVALUATE SUCCESS BY GETTING
EVERYONE ON BOARD. THEY CELEBRATE AND INVEST IN THOSE WHO RESPOND.

I want you to imagine something. Pretend you have a friend who just returned
from a hunting trip. It was his very first duck hunt. He was excited when he left
for the trip, knowing how much fun others had bagging ducks on this big lake. He
bought all the gear and was ready for the time of his life. As he walked through
the door upon returning home, you smile and ask, "Well—how was the hunt?"

He doesn't smile back. Something has obviously gone wrong. "The day was
terrible," he muses, proceeding to slump in a chair and pout. Assuming he didn't
get any ducks at all, you ask if he missed every shot he took. "Oh no—I actually
got twelve ducks. See, here they are," he said, immediately producing a bag of
twelve beautiful ducks. Now, you're just plain confused. When you bring up his
apparent success with these twelve, he looks up and responds, "Well, sure, I got
twelve ducks. But... hundreds of them got away!"

While this imaginary story seems far-fetched, there is a point to it. It's obvious to
anyone who has spent the day crouching in a duck blind, that you don't have to
get all the ducks to have a good hunt. Unlike the elk hunter, who reminisces about
the elk he missed, a returning duck hunter focuses on what he got. Because let's
face it, with just one gun and hundreds of ducks flying away, you're bound to miss
plenty of them. In other words, a good duck hunter might miss dozens of ducks
and still bag the limit! But if he keeps whining about the ones that got away, he
won't—in fact, he can't—last long in this sport.

Going after a duck is a deliberate act; so is the art of leading people. Good leaders
know their target. As a leader, you need to lead those who respond. No leader gets
all the "ducks." You can't focus on the "missed ducks." There will always be those
that got away. There will always be people who criticize you, or don't like you, or
didn't vote for you, or refuse to cooperate with you.

Whether you're the president of the student body on campus or the president of a corporation, you need to keep your eye on the people who respond. Those are the "ducks" you bag and you must deliberately invest in them.

I have taught this principle at multiple conferences already, and I usually learn something each time I do. I recently had a duck hunter come up to me after my session and talk with me about his duck hunting experience. "If you focus on all the ducks," he said, "you won't hit any of them." Maybe you will accidentally hit one or two, but it's all chance. In duck hunting, you are aiming at a moving target. You don't focus on the ducks that are hiding. You watch for the a duck that is flying in plain sight and focus on that one. Similarly, leaders cannot go after everyone. They must know precisely who they want to "catch" and target them.

This is one of my favorite principles. Why? Because I had to learn it the hard way. When I first was put in a leadership position, I was a people pleaser. I wanted everyone to like me. I thought I had to win everybody to "my side." If somebody came to me with a complaint, I immediately made a program change. I literally tried to please everyone, but realized the hard way, that wasn't realistic. No leader will ever please every person. Some may never "get with your program." And that's OK. Some may get upset with you, even hurt your feelings, but your job is to concentrate on those who respond to your invitation to go on the journey. Leaders must learn to live with "missed ducks." They must learn to celebrate the ones they get!

Charles Simeon served as a vicar at Holy Trinity Anglican Church in Cambridge for fifty-four years. When he arrived, many from his congregation didn't like him. He was ridiculed and insulted by church members. Some folks even tried to kick him out of the parish. They didn't understand him.

Simeon desperately wanted to impact the English culture, but the Anglican Church was unproductive and irrelevant to the needs of people. He realized that traditional methods would not produce the results he wanted, so he had to change his approach. He decided to go "duck hunting." He began to focus on the students across the street at Cambridge University. He signed up to speak in chapel as often as they would let him. After the chapels, he invited those students who were interested in further study to meet him later that week for a Conversation Group. Simeon taught this group on a deeper level. He watched those who responded and challenged them further. At these Conversation Groups, he carefully observed the young leaders who were most responsive. Knowing he couldn't invest in everyone, he chose about fifteen of these student leaders to equip one evening a week at something he called Supper Clubs. The Supper Clubs met around his big British dining room table for deeper discussion and mentoring. Charles would spend hours pouring his life into this handful of students. And at these Supper Clubs, he would zero in on about three to four seniors who would graduate soon. They became his "inner circle." Simeon prepared these few seniors to lead a church once they graduated.

During this period of history, the wealthy people determined who filled the pulpits of their churches. Because of their big donations—they chose who became the vicar at their church. Consequently, Charles Simeon began to raise funds so he could place his young, trained leaders in positions to lead in these Anglican churches and ultimately change the culture. He quietly continued this practice for 54 years. By the time Simeon died, he had equipped and placed 1,100 young men as leaders of churches in England. Literally, one third of all the Anglican churches were led by Simeon's army of young leaders! In addition, he impacted men like William Wilberforce, who devoted his life to the abolition of slavery in England. Charles Simeon reached hundreds of thousands of people by focusing on a few "ducks" at a time. Notice his strategy below:

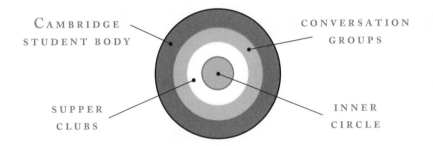

This principle is not about ignoring those who don't follow you. It's about challenging everyone to go on the journey with you—but investing in those who do. This principle isn't an excuse to have a tiny influence, or to ignore the masses or those who disagree with you. Even big rallies are the result of small networks that succeeded. The point, however, is that pouring into a core group actually increases your chances to move the masses. Leaders learn to overlook "missed ducks," knowing the few "committed ones" make the hunt successful.

REFLECT AND RESPOND

Reflect on some historical or contemporary leaders who clarified their mission and screened out some followers along the way. Jot down what you have learned about "duck hunting" from these leaders.

_____
_____
_____
_____
_____

Are you worried about "missed ducks?" Briefly explain.

_____

_____

_____

_____

Do you refuse to compromise the commitment it takes to lead effectively? What has motivated you to remain committed?

_____

_____

_____

_____

SELF-ASSESSMENT

Think about the last time you tried to rally people to do something. Remember something you really were excited to do. Rate yourself in the following areas:

How was the response?

_____

_____

_____

_____

If not everyone responded positively, ask yourself, did it bother me? Did it hurt me? Was I upset?

_____

_____

_____

_____

Did I clarify the vision or compromise it to get more people?

_____

_____

_____

_____

Was I focusing on the missed ducks? (Do I struggle with people pleasing?)

_____

_____

_____

_____

EXERCISE

As a leader, consider the next project in which you want to get people involved. Approach it like a duck hunt. Write out your responses to these questions:

1. Who is your target audience?

_____

_____

_____

_____

2. Who might be a small core group of responsive people you could invest in to create momentum? Select that core group and equip them to own the vision and participate with you in it.

_____

_____

_____

_____

3. Can you get excited about this core group?

_____

_____

_____

_____

4. Can you stop worrying about the "missed ducks" (the people who don't respond)?

_____

_____

_____

_____

IMAGE SEVEN
[Choir Director]

[CHOIR DIRECTOR]

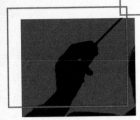

Choir Director

CHOIR DIRECTORS ARE A GOOD PICTURE OF LEADERSHIP AND TEAM BUILDING. THEY RECRUIT, AUDITION, ASSIGN PARTS, REHEARSE AND DIRECT MUSIC. BUT AT THE END OF THE PERFORMANCE, THE DIRECTOR MAKES SURE THE APPLAUSE GOES TO THE CHOIR.

I remember singing in a couple of choirs growing up. I sang in our middle school chorus, as well as a youth ensemble in high school. Both were fun, despite the fact that I can't sing. I'm serious. I don't have a good voice. I often tell people I'm known as a back-up singer—each time I approach a microphone, everyone says, "Back up!"

Looking back, I can see now what those choir directors were up to. They had plenty of girls in the choir, but needed more guys. So, they went after what they needed and worked with what they got. Both directors approached me, and asked if I'd sing in their choir. Both auditioned me, and for some reason, felt there was a place for my voice in the group. After all, it was a team, and I could blend with the others, right? They determined what part I could sing: tenor. (Tenor is right... "ten-or"- twelve notes off key!) Both choir directors spent extra time rehearsing with me, many times after the regular rehearsal was over. They put up with my mischievous sense of humor until I finally learned my part. After our performances were over, I remember getting standing ovations from the crowd. Imagine that. Not bad for a choir with a guy who can't sing. Today—I know better. I realize that no matter how good the choir sounds, standing ovations really belong to the director.

Dr. Johnson is the director of an outstanding collegiate choir. Every year, he auditions numerous men and women for the seventy-two-voice choir. And every year, many talented singers are turned away. You might even say many extremely talented singers do not meet the audition requirements. Why? Because Dr. Johnson isn't looking for outstanding soloists. The audition process entails more than just listening to individuals. He rehearses each person with everyone who sings that part, and does this for all eight parts. Having seventy-two soloists doesn't produce an outstanding choir.

Dr. Johnson's goal is to find seventy-two voices that blend together in pitch, style and harmony to create one unified sound that resonates like a pipe organ. Directors like Dr. Johnson know how to assemble a choir in order to achieve the sound they want. A choir director is a broker of talents.

Athletic coaches are a little like choir directors. You might be familiar with 1980 U.S. Olympic Hockey coach, Herb Brooks. He was portrayed by Kurt Russell in the 2004 movie, *Miracle*. In one scene, Brooks is observing players on the first day of tryouts with assistant coach Craig Patrick. Announcing that he's made his selection, Patrick is shocked. It's only the first day—AND—he's missing some of the best players on his list. Brooks tells him, "I'm not looking for the best players. I'm looking for the right players." Brooks knew everything about every one of the players trying out. He had talked to their coaches and watched tapes of their games. Brooks' coaching technique called for players who would work hard, play smart, and care more about the name on the front of the jersey than the one on the back. And those players weren't necessarily the best ones.

Brooks' hand-picked team went on to win the gold medal. They defeated the seasoned and unbeaten Soviet team—a nearly impossible task. Ken Morrow, one of the players on this team, described Brooks' coaching as, "an understanding of how to get the best out of each player and make him part of the team." Brooks built more than a team. He built a family.

The 2004 NBA championship is another example of a choir director. The L.A. Lakers were undeniably an all-star basketball team. They had Shaquille O'Neal, Kobe Bryant, Karl Malone and a truckload of others. They were stacked. The Detroit Pistons, on the other hand, were a team with "smaller-name" talent. As the season opened, the Pistons were ranked 9th, with the odds of winning the NBA title at 18 to 1. The Lakers were strong favorites to be champions again. Both teams made it to the NBA finals, but do you remember who won? The Pistons—the underdogs. Although the Lakers were overflowing with talent, it was an atmosphere thick with individualism and self-interest. Piston's coach, Larry Brown, knew that individuals may win trophies, but teams win championships. An article covering their win said, "The Pistons completed the biggest upset in NBA Finals history, toppling the mighty but misguided Los Angeles Lakers with a 100-87 victory that was entirely emblematic of a team triumphing over individuals." Larry Brown defined basketball as a sport that's about players playing the right way—showing you CAN be a team AND be successful. While the Lakers leaned heavily on their superstars, the Pistons shared both the ball and the spotlight. Fortunately for them, coach Brown was a choir director.

Good choir directors do something all good leaders must learn to do: team building. Effective leaders eventually recognize that their dreams are bigger than they are. In order to accomplish them, they must recruit a team whose personalities will blend well—just like a choir director recruits singers whose voices blend well. Soon, leaders realize they must equip their people for their role in fulfilling the dream.

First they recruit people based on character, competence and chemistry. Next they equip those people for their specific positions. Let's take a look at the process.

RECRUIT PLAYERS

Leaders who are "choir directors" don't let just anyone sing in the choir. Unlike my experience growing up, good directors look for three elements when they recruit:

CHARACTER—they look for honesty and discipline, instead of hoping it will come later.

COMPETENCE—they find people with the abilities they need who can deliver the goods.

CHEMISTRY—they recruit people who fit the personality and culture of the group.

AUDITION & ASSIGN PARTS

Deciding who meets the audition requirements involves getting familiar with the candidates. Good leaders explore the strengths, track record and passion of potential candidates. Positions are assigned based on the GIFTS of the person:

G – GIFTED.
    Leaders discover where the candidate's greatest gifts, talents, and values lie.

I - INFLUENTIAL.
    They discover where the candidate's deepest influence exists.

F – FRUITFUL.
    They discover where the candidate's greatest results will be achieved.

T – TRUSTWORTHY.
    They discover how much the candidate can be trusted on the job.

S – SERVICE.
    They discover where the candidate most wants to serve and invest their life.

CREATE HARMONY

Effective leaders don't leave harmony and healthy relationships to chance. They foster it with helpful team building exercises, bringing choir members together and encouraging them to help each other. Leaders build trust and alignment.

They create bridges of relationship that can bear the weight of the principles they value. Choir members don't sing the same notes, but together they create perfect harmony.

Rehearse & Prepare

Great vision without great people is irrelevant. Great leaders spend time preparing the choir for the "performance." They get the team ready for the game. They equip and resource the members with whatever is needed to get the job done. I suggest you equip your people using the following acrostic, IDEA, for your training:

I – Instruction.
  Verbally teach them the principles they need to know.

D – Demonstration.
  Model for them the desired results.

E – Experience.
  Launch them into participation, giving them on-the-job training.

A – Assessment.
  Offer them helpful feedback through evaluation.

Direct Them

When leadership guru Peter Drucker was asked to explain the most important question a leader can ask, he leaned against the table, lowered his head, and rocked a little. After a few minutes of silence, he looked up. "Who... does... what?" he said in a slow, deliberate voice. I agree. And I would add a second question: "Where are we going?" (Stephen Covey writes that only 17% of employees know exactly where their organization is going.) Answering these two questions provides the direction.

Deflect the Applause

Do you know what Herb Brooks did when his Olympic hockey team won the gold medal? He left the ice. Why? "It was not my spot," Brooks said in an interview. He wanted to leave the applause to his players—to those who deserved it. The glory of the victory went to the team. Brooks was a "choir director" who knew it was the singers, not the director, who needed to be recognized.

Reflect and Respond

In this *Habitude*, we looked at three elements to look for when recruiting a team: 1) Character 2) Competence 3) Chemistry. As you reflect on your team, identify how these three elements come into play—both positively and negatively—in the day-to-day operations of your team.

_____

_____

_____

_____

Self-Assessment

On a scale of 1 to 10, assess yourself as a choir director:

1. I identify and recruit the right people for the team:

   < POOR 1   2   3   4   5   6   7   8   9   10 EXCELLENT >

2. I accurately evaluate their strengths and passion:

   < POOR 1   2   3   4   5   6   7   8   9   10 EXCELLENT >

3. I'm good at placing people in their area of strength:

   < POOR 1   2   3   4   5   6   7   8   9   10 EXCELLENT >

4. I align the jobs of team members, so they work in harmony:

   < POOR 1   2   3   4   5   6   7   8   9   10 EXCELLENT >

5. I prepare my team to win by equipping and encouraging them:

   < POOR 1   2   3   4   5   6   7   8   9   10 EXCELLENT >

6. I provide clear direction to my players, both individually and as a team:

   < POOR 1   2   3   4   5   6   7   8   9   10 EXCELLENT >

7. I enjoy passing the credit for success to team members:

   < POOR 1   2   3   4   5   6   7   8   9   10 EXCELLENT >

Exercise

Select an event that you normally wouldn't be in charge of planning. It could be as crazy as New Year's Eve in Times Square, or as ordinary as a third grade field trip. You will need to find people to help you run different aspects of your event. Make a list of all the areas that need someone in charge. Do a mental "walk-through" of the event. How would you go about selecting the right people for the specific jobs you've chosen? How would you effectively equip them? How would you build harmony?

IMAGE EIGHT
[Taxi Principle]

Taxi Principle

ALWAYS ASK THE PRICE BEFORE YOU GET INTO A CAB. LEADERS COUNT THE COST BEFORE THEY BEGIN THE JOURNEY: PEOPLE, MONEY, TIME, AND ENERGY. WE MUST SIZE UP THE COST AND PREPARE BEFORE WE START DOWN A ROAD.

I travel quite a bit to New York City. In fact, I'm in big cities all over the world, from Manila to London, from Hong Kong to Prague to Buenos Aires. I learned something early on as I climbed into musty, humid taxicabs in those major metropolitan areas. Many of the cab drivers want to take you for a ride—in more ways than one.

I've spent major bucks on rides through town, simply because I didn't discuss the price, or route, beforehand. I've seen drivers take the longest route possible, just to hike up the price. So, at this point in my life, I try to follow a little rule. I stand outside the cab, and talk to the driver about these things before I ever get into the car. That way, if I choose to get into the cab, I've removed as many surprises as possible.

If you haven't grown up in a big city, you may not be aware of the term, gypsy cab. Basically, it's a "fake cab" that will make a round-about trip to your destination for an obscenely high price. So if you haven't stumbled upon any gypsy cabs, consider yourself warned! A friend was telling me of a time he was overseas and fell into the gypsy cab trap. He and some buddies got into what they thought was a cab, but when they got out, they were nowhere near their intended destination. So, they got into another cab for the second leg of their journey. They eventually got to their destination, but arrived with empty wallets.

Humorist Lewis Grizzard unintentionally touched upon this Taxi Principle on one of his tours. "I asked a bellman outside a Miami hotel to call me a cab. It was late in the evening. Just then, I noticed a cab parked across the street. 'Never mind,' I said to the bellman. 'There's a cab across the street.' 'No, no,' said the bellman. 'That is a fake cab. You get inside, and the driver takes off somewhere and beats you up and takes your money.'" Oops. Fortunately for Grizzard, someone knew the high cost of that journey and gave him a heads up.

Most of our time is so focused on reaching our destination or goal, we forget about how we're going to get there.

It's been said, "The longer the line of preparation, the more likely it is to intersect the line of opportunity." While preparation may not require years for every situation, it does require you to stop before you begin. If you take the time to plan and prepare for your journey, you'll save yourself numerous struggles. This applies to taxi cabs in a small way. It applies to leadership in a big way. Always count the cost before you get in.

Charles Lindbergh, or "Lucky Lindy," was the first man to fly solo across the Atlantic Ocean. But he didn't just "take-off" one day on a whim. Lindbergh knew that any task, especially one as big as this, took preparation. While his plane, "The Spirit of St. Louis," was being built, Lindbergh prepared. His friend Frank Samuels recalled a time when he and Lindbergh flew to San Diego to check on the plane's progress. Waking up during the night, he looked over to see Lindbergh's bed was empty. As his eyes adjusted to the darkness of the hotel room, he noticed him sitting by the window. Samuels asked what he was doing up at that hour? "Just practicing," replied Lindbergh. Practicing? What could possibly be practiced by gazing at the stars? "Staying awake all night." Lindbergh knew his flight would require being alert for an extended period of time, and he prepared mentally and also physically.

Others had attempted the flight between New York and Paris, but no one had succeeded. Some had even ended drastically. When Lindbergh took off, he equipped himself with four sandwiches, two canteens of water, and 451 gallons of gasoline. He'd done a "mental walk-through" of the trip several times, calculating all that could happen. During his flight, sleet began to cling to the plane. "That worried me a great deal," Lindbergh noted in his journal, "and I debated whether I should keep on or go back. I decided I must not think anymore about going back." He knew the trip may cost him his life, but he'd counted the cost beforehand. Because of his preparation, Lindbergh was able to remain calm and choose a wise course of action. He succeeded because he practiced the taxi principle.

THE MENTAL WALK THROUGH AND NEXT STEPS

Many times, the preparation we put into an event far exceeds the amount of time we're actually at the event. (It may take hours to prepare a twenty-minute speech!) This is where a "mental walk-through" comes in handy. Charles Lindbergh flew that plane across the Atlantic mentally, before he did so physically. Furthermore, he experienced many of the hazards inwardly before facing them as realities. As you lead people, projects and events—practice the mental walk through whenever possible. For instance, before the big social event you're planning, attend it in your head. Walk through the doors of the building. Is everything in place? Where are the cups and napkins—how about the greeters? As you size up what's needed, ask yourself: Can we pull this off with excellence? Is it worth the cost? And if so, what do I need to do to make it happen?

Whenever you participate in a planning meeting, write every action step down, making sure every base is covered. Then, recognize that the most important item to come out of that meeting will be "next steps." What are the next action-steps needed to make progress? Who will take them? When?

In April of 1988, a news program did a feature on a photographer who was also a skydiver. He often combined his two skills and filmed groups of skydivers jumping from planes. The film shown on the telecast was different from any the photographer had taken before. As the final skydiver opened his chute, the picture went berserk. The broadcaster reported that the cameraman had fallen to his death, having jumped out of the plane without his parachute. It wasn't until he reached for the ripcord that he realized he was free-falling without one. He'd forgotten to pack it.

Until that moment, the jump was probably exciting and fun. But tragically, the photographer prepared to film the fall, but failed to prepare for the fall. His faith was in a parachute that was never buckled to his back. How many times do we lead like this? Whether it's a meeting, a test, or your job, there is always a price to pay for lack of preparation.

REFLECT AND RESPOND

We looked at two key principles for leaders to consider before they attempt to reach their goals:

    1. Count the cost   2. Preparation

Jot down how you have (or have not) implemented these two elements in your leadership. What was the end result?

_____

_____

Charles Lindbergh prepared for his solo flight across the Atlantic Ocean by doing "a mental walk through" of the trip several times before the actual flight. Describe the benefits of walking through an event in your head before the actual event.

_____

_____

How could this practice help you avoid pitfalls as you lead people, projects or events?

_____

_____

Self-Assessment

Based on the following questions, assess yourself on the taxi principle:

Where do I need to go? (Find your target)

_____

How "far-out" is my goal? (Assess the distance)

_____

What are the conditions? (Factor in any adversities)

_____

What will it take to get there? (Select your tools)

_____

Am I willing to pay the price? (Count the cost)

_____

Exercise

Some night this week, put $10 in your pocket and leave your wallet/checkbook/credit card at home. This solitary ten-dollar bill needs to feed you and two friends for the next four meals. How do you approach the situation? How will you go about feeding three people, four times? Can you make it? Come up with a plan. If you're ambitious, put your plan into action and see how well you planned.

A final warning: Robert F. Scott and Roald Amundsen were both explorers. These two men are a contrast in leadership. Scott resolved to be the first man to reach the South Pole. His team set out in 1910, but was ill prepared for the journey—and suffered because of it. On January 17th, 1912, they became the second team to reach the pole. Even worse, Scott failed to prepare for the return home. His team was low on food and fuel, causing them enormous hardship. A deadly blizzard left them just eleven miles short of a supply depot. Their remains were found the following spring. Roald Amundsen, on the other hand, quietly and secretly set aim for the South Pole. He planned every aspect of the expedition, maximizing his chances for success. On December 14th, 1911, with a team of expert skiers and dog teams, Amundsen made the feat—he reached the South Pole (and did so 34 days before Scott!). The difference in these two stories was preparation. Successful preparation begins with knowing "what you want" and "what you're willing to pay."

Barn Building

A FARMER BUILDS THE BARN ON HIS PROPERTY FIRST. WHY? BECAUSE THE BARN WILL PAY FOR ALL OF THE OTHER STRUCTURES. LEADERS DETERMINE THE CRITICAL TRANSACTION THAT ENABLES EVERYTHING ELSE TO HAPPEN.

A farmer and his wife purchased some new property. They were excited about moving and settling down on this new land. It was just perfect. A dream-come-true. One evening at dinner, the two of them began discussing hopes and dreams for their piece of real estate. Soon, it became apparent they needed to come up with a plan for what they would build, and when. They both wanted to build a house, a silo, a three-car garage, a shed, a swing-set and a barn. They were passionate about each structure, but which should come first?

The decision was finally reduced to either the house or the barn. The wife wanted to build the house first. She could envision just how the living room would be decorated and how the kitchen would be laid-out. She knew the color schemes, the window treatments and the furniture she wanted. The farmer had to admit, it sounded great! He listened quietly and pondered her words. But when she finished, he smiled and said they shouldn't build the house first. He felt they should build the barn first. She was shocked. "Why?" she asked. "Aren't we more important than the animals?" They went back and forth in disagreement. Their argument finally ended when the farmer played the "trump card." He said, "Sweetheart, we have to build the barn first—because the barn will build the house."

Do you understand how profound these words were? Like his wife, if you were developing a farm, the first item you may think you need is a house. That's where you eat, sleep, and live. Sounds logical, right? But any wise farmer would suggest a different plan. Build the barn. The house is "overhead." The barn is the hub of all of the profit-making work. The animals live there, so it produces your milk, eggs, and meat. The equipment stored there is necessary for working the fields and growing crops. Without the barn, the farm could generate little income. If you neglect the barn and build only the house, the house is all you'll get. Build the barn, and you can build a house, shed, silo, chicken coop, and even another barn—you can build pretty much anything!

These days, the number of private farms is dwindling because of technology. When it was more standard, however, it wasn't uncommon for families to live in their barn. Building it was a large expense, and many times families had to save more money before they could build their actual house. Living in the barn was an easy and affordable option. Half of the barn was reserved for the animals, while the other half served as their living accommodations. Prior to 1900, such a practice was relatively normal as families waited to build their house.

While living in a barn has become rare these days, there are still many instances where families sacrifice the comforts of a house, in order to develop security for the family. I read a story about Becki Neal and her sister Judy who moved to Sisters, Oregon in 1978 to open a beauty salon. For the first nine months, the two women and Judy's two teenage sons lived in tents. Financing the salon was their first priority, and they didn't have enough money to also build a house. Eventually, they wanted horses. They still didn't have a house, but you know what they did? They built the barn and finished half of it for living quarters! Wow. Talk about sacrifice. But they were shrewd; they knew how to reach their goals swiftly and wisely.

In almost every endeavor, there is a "barn," or an activity that is vital to the life of the project or organization. In business, it's called the "critical transaction." It's the activity that if you don't do it, you're "out of business." On a farm, the barn represents the critical transaction. Without the barn, the life of the farm cannot be sustained. Similarly, the critical transaction of an airline is not when the plane takes off, but when the customer buys the ticket. A radio station's critical transaction is not choosing what songs to play, but selling airtime for commercials. When people don't buy, businesses don't run, planes can't take off, and songs cannot play.

Organizations that discover their critical transaction have a better chance of succeeding. While many companies provide numerous products, almost every company has one they feature as "their" product. Many big name companies are thriving, simply because they've discovered their critical transaction. Hewlett-Packard makes computers, digital cameras, and scanners, but they're known for their printers. Ketchup made Heinz 57 famous, but did you know that they also produce bagel bites and baby food? Xerox discovered its niche in the world of heavy-duty office copiers, but continues to produce scanners and computer monitors on a smaller scale. This "Barn Building" *Habitude* complements the other images you read about earlier, like "Rivers and Floods" and "Bit Market." The "Rivers and Floods" *Habitude* teaches us to narrow and clarify our vision. "Bit Market" reminds us not to confuse our methods with our mission. This Barn Building *Habitude* helps us zero in on the one activity that helps every other activity to happen. There are three criteria for finding your "barn":

GENERATES REVENUE:
What brings in the most income so everything else can happen?

CREATES MOMENTUM:
What sparks movement and excitement toward your mission?

ENABLES ACTIVITY:
What is the catalyst for all other activities on your team?

The concept of finding your "barn" works beyond finding a product that will earn money and a name. Any group of people working toward a purpose should discover their critical transaction. In 2000, the film *Remember the Titans* illustrated how one man taught his team how to play football. Coach Herman Boone, an African-American, was faced with the difficult challenge of coaching a team of African-Americans and Caucasians. Racial prejudice still existed in his small, Virginia town. Boone knew the critical transaction moved beyond the realms of football. It involved breaking racial barriers and building healthy relationships. Without that camaraderie, Boone knew the team's performance on the field would suffer. And if the team failed, this would only add another roadblock toward gaining equal rights. Coach Boone centered on this critical transaction with his athletes, and everything else took care of itself. Good leaders always find the one catalyst that makes everything else happen.

REFLECT AND RESPOND

Reflect on your leadership responsibilities. Choose one specific area and describe your "critical transaction." In other words, what is the one catalyst that makes everything else happen, that is vital to the life of a project or your organization?

_____
_____
_____
_____

The critical transaction of an airline is not when the plane takes off, but when the customer buys the ticket. Planes can't take off if tickets aren't purchased. Illustrate how it is possible to forget what really produces.

_____
_____
_____
_____

Why do you think we get distracted from focusing on the critical transaction?

_____
_____
_____
_____

Self-Assessment

With the following questions, assess yourself on how well you know and practice "barn building" in your organization:

What one function could either make or break me as a leader?

_____

_____

What one function can either make or break my team (organization)?

_____

_____

Discover your critical transaction:

_____

_____

What generates the most revenue?

_____

_____

What sparks the most momentum?

_____

_____

What enables the activities of the rest of the team?

_____

_____

Exercise

List all of the activities your organization performs. Then, jot down how each activity relies upon the others. (Drawing a chart of the relationship between all activities might be helpful). Is there one activity that seems to be the hub of the wheel—the one around which all others revolve?

To make this exercise more vivid, sit down with your team and pretend you're starting a new program from scratch. You have no money—only ideas. Once you come up with it, ask yourself: what must we focus on to generate the money and excitement needed to get this off the ground?

Small Sprocket

LEADERS ARE THE SMALL SPROCKETS IN EFFECTING CHANGE. WE MUST SPIN
DOZENS OF TIMES BEFORE THE BIG GEAR MAKES ONE REVOLUTION. IT'S PART
OF THE TERRITORY. SPIN LIKE CRAZY AND EVENTUALLY OTHERS WILL RESPOND.

As a high school student, I rode my bike to school—at least until I got a car.
Riding my bike was memorable because I had to ride up a huge hill called "Fletcher
Parkway." It was a solid, three-quarter mile, uphill climb. Every morning, I was
sweating by the time I reached the top. Thank Schwinn for ten-speed bikes! Shifting
into low gear was my only hope. (As you know, low gears allow a biker to climb hills
when there's no momentum). My trade-off was pedaling like crazy just to move a
few feet.

I suppose it's a little like a car. When you drive, the engine revs between 1,000 and
3,000 RPMs (revolutions per minute), depending on the momentum you have. In
other words, a car's motor spins thousands of revolutions each moment, only to
move your tires down the road just one, short mile! It's a small wheel moving a big
wheel—a tiny gear spinning frantically, to move the larger one just a bit. It's the Law
of Leverage... and it illustrates the principle of the Small Sprocket.

Imagine two sprockets. One small one, one big one. It's the job of the small sprocket
to turn the big sprocket. If the small sprocket is half the size of the big one, it must
go around twice before the big one completes a full revolution. Doesn't sound too
bad, does it? Now imagine that small sprocket is 100th the size of the big one. Now
it must rotate 100 times in order to make the big sprocket complete a full revolution!

That's how life is for the leader of an organization. Sometimes things flow smoothly
and you don't feel like you're working too hard. Then there are times (and these are
more common) when you have to work, work, work, work, work—just to feel like
the team is progressing at all! You spin and spin and spin in order to accomplish all
of your leadership tasks. You keep communicating the vision, but everyone still seems
fuzzy on it. You tell them what needs to be done, but they need a reminder. You equip
them to recruit a team, but they continue to be a one-man show. You labor and labor...
anticipating seeing some result.

It can be discouraging. It feels like you've moved ahead fifty miles, but the group is moving like an inchworm! How can this be?

Relax. It's normal. Welcome to leadership. Leaders must spin like a small sprocket to get the larger group to spin just once. It can be tiresome. At first, the labor ratio is often disproportionate. But just wait. Continue spinning. Good news is coming. People will eventually respond to your spinning. And you know what? Once you really get moving and have the group responding positively, that big sprocket starts picking up speed from its own momentum. In time, the group will be spinning you!

You may remember the 2000 movie, *Pay It Forward*. Based on a true story, Trevor McKinney creates the "pay it forward" idea as a social studies project in school. The breakdown is pretty simple: do something to help someone, then ask them to do the same for three other individuals. Don't pay the kindness back; pay it forward. The whole movie is about Trevor helping people and trying to inspire them to pay it forward. His project seems to be failing, as Trevor spins and spins... and nobody seems to join his quest to make the world a better place. He is ready to give up.

In the end, Trevor learns that he started a movement. From homeless people to corporate CEOs, his good deeds and their forward momentum reached so many people that they caught the attention of a reporter. The truth is, Trevor had been spinning a long time before he saw any results. In his eyes, the big sprocket hadn't moved. But in reality, it was actually just picking up momentum. Hearing that his project was successful re-ignited Trevor's original desire to share kindness in the world. In the movie, there were increased random acts of kindness throughout the region. In real life, however, the movie inspired the creation of the "Pay It Forward" movement. People are paying it forward from Washington to Florida, all the way to Singapore and Australia.

In 1809, a boy named Louie was born in a small town near Paris. His early years consisted of many difficult obstacles. Playing with his father's tools one day, Louie pierced and destroyed his left eye. Shortly after that, his damaged eye infected the other, causing complete loss of sight in both eyes. While most blind people at the time became beggars, Louie wanted to attend school. So at the age of ten, he enrolled in a school for the blind. Students were taught to read raised letters, but due to the difficult process, only 14 books were available to study. Louie knew there had to be an easier way and set about creating a finger alphabet.

He began creating a system that would allow every blind person to read, write and communicate. Early on, it had little success because the system was too complex for kids to master. But Louie experimented with more simplified systems over the next few months, finally arriving at the ideal "six dot" system. By the time he was fifteen, Louie had developed separate codes for math and music.

Although his creation had improved life for blind people, it didn't catch on. Sighted people didn't understand how the dot system could be useful. One teacher even banned children from learning it.

Eventually—after years of spinning like crazy—folks realized the benefits of the system. Today, the Braille System has been adapted to almost every known language, from Albanian to Zulu. Against all odds, Louie became an independent man and even went on to become a teacher in his old school.

As a young leader, I remember trying to start new projects in the organization where I was employed. I thought my ideas were great, but few others agreed. After all, I was the new kid on the block and I was young. Fortunately, there were a few of us who began spinning like small sprockets. We knew we couldn't spin wildly in all directions, so we consistently spun like crazy in one direction. I'd look in the mirror each day and say, "I'm a small sprocket!" Over time, momentum picked up. Management saw that our ideas had potential, and we were given the go ahead to begin implementing some of them. By the time I left that job, we were successful in reaching all of our original goals.

We were small sprockets. As leaders, if we don't have the courage and determination to keep spinning, things will grind to a halt. Very little will change. In fact, the vision will shrivel and the team will likely suffer. It's the leader's job to spin like crazy and fire up the rest of the team. It's part of the territory of leadership. Fueled by determination, leaders are the engines. We are the small sprockets.

Reflect and Respond

In the world of nature, we can learn a lot about the small sprocket principle from the ant, a small creature. Their highly organized colonies often consist of millions of individual ants, yet they appear to operate as a single entity. They work in teams to move extremely heavy things. They gather food during harvest and store it until the winter months. Without an administrator, they perform specific jobs as workers, soldiers, drones and queens. Yet, when a catastrophe occurs, the ants quickly adapt their duties to overcome the problem.

Summarize the characteristics that enable the ant to succeed:

_____

_____

Contrast the ant's initiative and perseverance with our own human laziness. Why do we often fail to persevere? What prevents our "spinning?"

_____

_____

Self-Assessment

Evaluate yourself on the following three qualities that we find in an ant's work ethic.

1. INTEGRITY: THE ANT DOESN'T NEED SUPERVISION. IT WORKS BECAUSE IT IS THE RIGHT THING TO DO.

   Have you ever been in a program that seemed stagnant? What kept it from making progress?

   _____

   _____

   _____

2. INITIATIVE: THE ANT STARTS TO GATHER FOOD WITHOUT BEING PUSHED. IT DOESN'T NEED SOMEONE TO SHOW IT THE WAY.

   In your activities, do you ever feel alone in doing all the work? How do you typically respond?

   _____

   _____

   _____

3. INDUSTRY: THE ANT HAS A SPIRIT OF INDUSTRY. IT WORKS AND WORKS UNTIL THE JOB IS DONE.

   How do you stay inspired when you don't see results and you don't feel any gratification?

   _____

   _____

   _____

EXERCISE

Choose a cause that you believe needs to be promoted on your campus or in your organization. Determine to take six months and actively promote this cause. Choose two or three actions you can take that would strategically help people understand and support the cause. Then—do them. Spin like crazy. Evaluate at the end of six months. Do you see any improvement? Will it take more time?

You may remember the story about two mice that fell into a milk pail. The sides of the bucket were too steep for the mice to climb out, and the milk wasn't deep enough for them to scurry over the edge. So the pair began to tread milk, desperately trying to stay alive. After awhile, one of them grew weary and stopped. He gave up. As a result, the mouse drowned in the milk. The second one, however, kept treading. His little legs paddled and paddled and paddled. Eventually, his ceaseless paddling churned the milk into butter, solid enough to climb upon. Like a small sprocket, that second mouse kept spinning. His unrelenting treading eventually provided a place to stand.

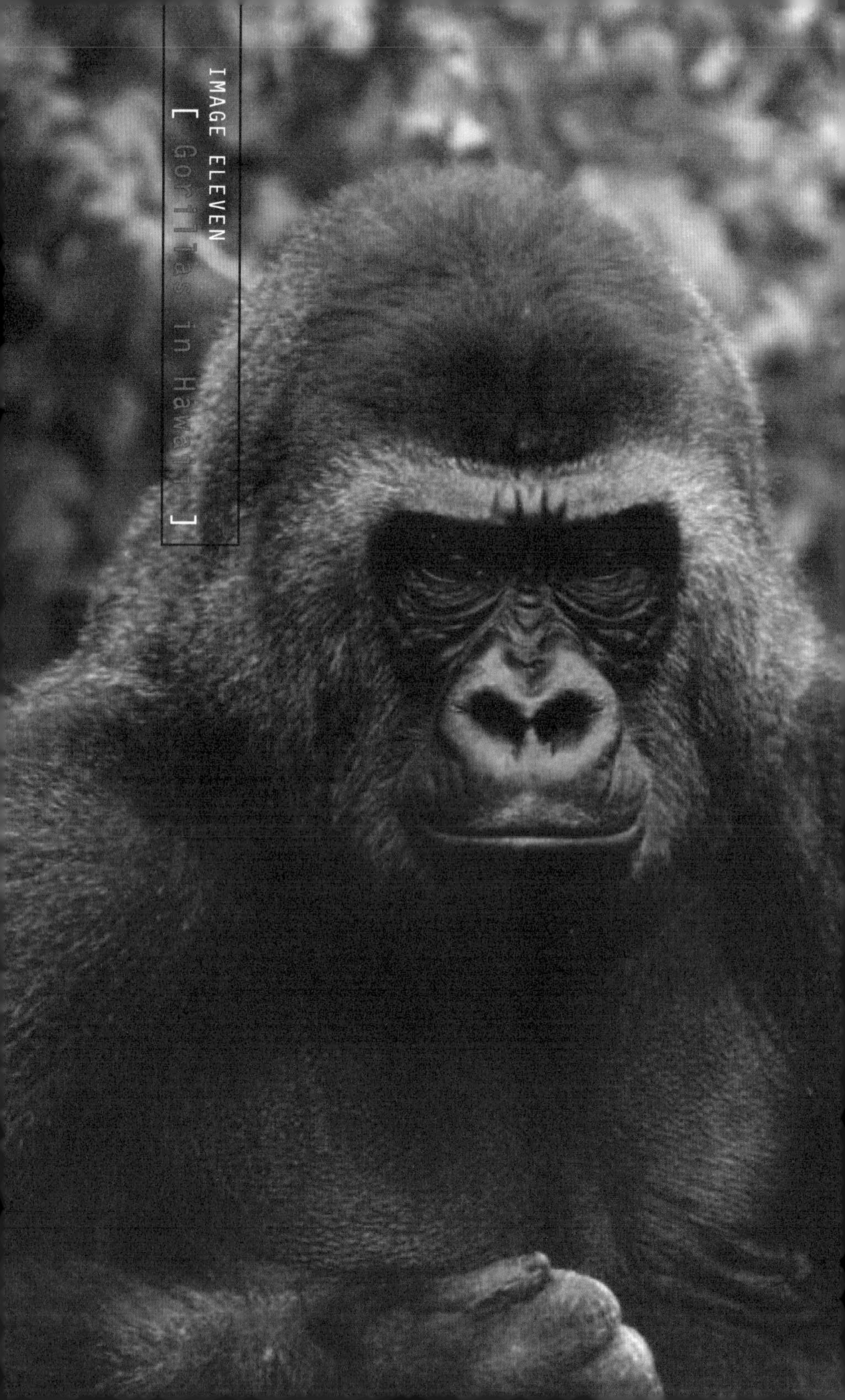

IMAGE ELEVEN

[Gorillas in Hawaii]

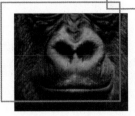

Gorillas in Hawaii

NO MATTER HOW BIG OR IMPOSSIBLE THE TASK, LEADERS FIND A WAY TO GET THE JOB DONE. THEIR PASSION HELPS THEM TO BE CREATIVE AND THEIR PERSISTENCE ENABLES THEM TO FINISH WHAT THEY START, WHATEVER IT TAKES.

Do you ever get asked to do things that just seem impossible? My good friend David likes to tell about an unusual assignment he once got on his job. During college, he worked at a company that produced commercials for big-name companies. As you can imagine, photo shoots can call for the use of all kinds of "props." David's boss called him one day during class. They were going to do a photo shoot for a truck ad in Hawaii—and they needed a gorilla. David's task was to locate a gorilla and figure out how to get it to Hawaii. He had no gorilla experience and, unfortunately, the book *How To Locate and Transport a Gorilla For Dummies* had never been published. David spent the entire day on the phone. It's not often you hear a classmate saying, "No, I need a silverback gorilla."

Ultimately, David made contact with the animal trainer at Michael Jackson's personal zoo. This man knew how to transport apes. Finally, David got some answers. He hit a financial wall when he learned how expensive it is to transport a gorilla by plane. Not only would a private plane need to be hired, but they also needed to hire a trained crew. Who knew you couldn't fly a gorilla in economy class?! David discovered helicopters to be more cost effective. Before long, David's persistence paid off, and he was able to call his boss with all of the answers. Despite the difficult task and dead ends he hit along the way, David figured out how to get a gorilla to Hawaii. He got the job done.

This is a picture of what great leaders confront on a regular basis. David's challenge was one he'd never faced before. There was no manual, so he had to learn as he went about the task. He "built the bridge as he crossed it." Finding gorillas wasn't on David's job description, but he never complained that it was someone else's job. He just smiled and got creative.

By definition, leaders will take their teams into new territory. They don't just maintain the status quo. Because the territory is new, there is no protocol; there is no guide telling them what to do next.

Sometimes leaders have to feel their way through the pitch-black cave with their hands. You can't always tell where you'll land when you take your next step, but sooner or later you will see some light in the cave. David had to start off with guessing when he made his first call. Eventually, the phone calls and websites shed light on his path. As a leader, you have to start somewhere and move forward from there. But once you start, make sure you finish.

According to the rules of baseball, you have to leave the batter's box after your third strike. There's no such rule in the game of life. Attempting to complete a task, you may quickly reach your "third strike." You may go from one dead-end to another, while attempting to find your gorilla. If you're smart though, you'll continue swinging until you finally hit the grand slam. The game isn't over until you step out of the batter's box. As leaders, once we step into that box, we must keep on swinging. Sometimes that will mean swinging at a pitch that looks impossible to hit. But it may also mean being surprised when you nick a curve ball that gets you to first base. If a pitch has any potential to provide you with answers, swing at it!

Hamilton Wright Mable said, "Don't worry about opposition. Remember, a kite rises against the wind, not with the wind." We need to approach challenges with this same mindset. At first, it may seem like a hindrance, but in the end, the wind is what allows the kite to soar and dip gracefully across the sky. Without the wind, the beauty within the kite is not revealed. Face the challenge head-on, with passion, and allow it to help you soar. Remember, no one rises to meet low expectations.

While I was in college, I mentored a group of middle school and high school students. Several of the teens in our group were big fans of the heavy metal band, KISS. While I understood their fascination with the wild gimmicks of Gene Simmons, over and over I saw the negative influence of that band on those young students. Those kids were intrigued with the celebrity life of drugs, sex and money. One night, I found myself wishing that someone would do something about the influence of KISS on middle school kids! Before the night was over, I knew I was that someone. I couldn't just wish about the situation any longer. I had to do more.

To make a long story short, KISS did a concert in town later that year. I did some homework to find out what hotel they'd be staying in, what their routines were on-site and even prepared some material to give them. The front desk clerk at the hotel wasn't about to cooperate and tell me what room they were staying in, so I spoke to the hotel maids until one of them confided where they were. I waited until midnight before I saw a man standing outside their door. He was their bouncer. When I asked him if I could speak with the band members, he told me it was his job to keep people like me away. So—I offered him the material I'd prepared and asked if he'd give it to the band. At that moment, he realized I was no groupie. I was concerned about the teens in that town, and wanted to talk to KISS about them. Sensing my passion, he leaned down and whispered where I could find all four band members later that night. At 2:00 a.m., they sauntered down to the bar in that hotel, and I was waiting.

The bouncer let me speak with them in person. We had an excellent conversation about their influence on teens. Mission accomplished. Granted, reaching that simple goal didn't change the world, but it was an adventure in attempting something I couldn't pull off easily. I had to take the initiative. There was no manual or job description. It was a little like getting a gorilla to Hawaii.

At times you will fail in attempting a gorilla-sized task. Failure is part of life. Giving up, however, isn't. Just ask R. H. Macy. He failed seven times before his store in New York caught on. Novelist John Creasey received 753 rejection slips before he published the first of his 564 books. Thomas Edison was thrown out of school in the early grades when the teachers decided he couldn't do the work. And, when Bob Dylan performed at a high school talent show, his classmates booed him off the stage. Eventually, these people were all successful because they didn't give up when they failed. Gorillas in Hawaii. This *Habitude* is about being proactive, being passionate, and being persistent. The next time you're assigned an impossible task, remember the words painted above the doorway to the Pittsburgh Steelers' locker room: "Whatever it takes."

REFLECT AND RESPOND

Do you have a cause that you'd give your life for, in order to fulfill it? If so, what is that cause?

_____

_____

Do you know someone who has a "whatever it takes" attitude? What enabled him or her to keep this attitude and finish well?

_____

_____

In what areas of your leadership is it toughest to maintain a "whatever it takes" attitude?

_____

_____

SELF-ASSESSMENT

Reflect on an overwhelming task that you've faced. Evaluate yourself based on the following qualities:

1. LEADERS ARE PROACTIVE.
   How did you handle it? Did you shrink from the challenge? Did you wait for someone else to begin?

   _____

   _____

2. LEADERS ARE PASSIONATE.
   Did you complain that it's not in your job description? Did you hesitate not knowing what to do?

   _____

   _____

3. LEADERS ARE PERSISTENT.
   Was it difficult to stick with it until the job got done? Did you give up when the going got tough?

   _____

   _____

4. What gorillas are you currently facing? Identify them. Create a plan for getting these gorillas to Hawaii!

   _____

   _____

EXERCISE

Sit down tonight and watch the news. While you're watching, choose one reported crisis and write down all of the details shared about this problem. If you were in charge of it, how would you solve it? Assume leadership over the situation and jot down what steps you would take to remedy the crisis, from start to finish.

_____

_____

_____

Take a break for ten minutes. Now, go back to what you jotted down. Evaluate the steps. Did you leave anything out? Is your solution realistic? Did you diagnose the problem accurately? Finally, are there any steps that you could take to actually implement this solution?

_____

_____

_____

IMAGE TWELVE

[The Starfield Principle]

IMAGE TWELVE

[The Star Trek Principle]

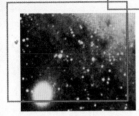

The Star Trek Principle

VIEWERS FOLLOWED THE STARSHIP ENTERPRISE BECAUSE IT BOLDLY WENT
WHERE NO MAN HAD GONE BEFORE. LEADERS INITIATE AND SET STANDARDS.
THEY HAVE A COMPASS IN THEIR HEAD AND A MAGNET IN THEIR HEART.

*Space. The final frontier. These are the voyages of the starship Enterprise.
Its five-year mission: to explore strange new worlds, to seek out new life and
new civilizations, to boldly go where no man has gone before...*

What premiered as a show destined to fail has become a worldwide obsession.
Gene Roddenberry, creator of *Star Trek*, went through two pilot episodes before
NBC decided to air the premiere on September 8, 1966. "The Man Trap," the
first episode, was a flop for sponsors. The series was so disappointing NBC
almost cancelled the show in December, only three months after it began. Ratings
for seasons two and three didn't show much improvement, and NBC aborted
Enterprise's five-year mission with the final episode on June 3, 1969.

The next month, the world watched astronaut Neil Armstrong's first lunar walk.
Mankind had landed on the moon. The series was sold to various TV networks that
continued to air the episodes. Soon people were demanding memorabilia from the
series. *Star Trek* conventions appeared in 1972 and over the next thirty years, eight
movies were produced, four additional series aired, and a letter campaign inspired
NASA to name an American space shuttle after the USS Enterprise.

So what turned this TV-series flop into a worldwide obsession? There are a
couple of reasons. First, *Star Trek* was not designed as mindless entertainment.
Roddenberry sought to create thought-provoking entertainment that was socially
relevant. Second, I think it strikes a chord of human desire. Consider the opening
words of the program: "To boldly go where no man has gone before." There's
something inside everyone that hungers to experience new territory, to explore new
places and to set new standards. It's no wonder over 53% of the American public
considers themselves *Star Trek* fans, or "Trekkies". Captain Kirk and the crew of
the Enterprise led the public to the unexplored galaxies!

This TV show illustrates another leadership principle. Leaders are like the starship Enterprise. They go first. They initiate and take new territory. In fact, this is the chief difference between "leaders" and "managers." Managers maintain the vision and organize the people. Leaders cast the vision and set the pace for others to follow. Managers maintain the territory that's already been taken. Leaders take new territory.

Roger Bannister was a little like the cast of *Star Trek*. Unless you're an educated runner, you may not be familiar with this name. In 1954, Bannister was the first person to run a mile in under four minutes! Pretty amazing. In 1939, Glenn Cunningham, the current world record miler, claimed the four-minute mile was beyond human effort. The world assumed he was right. It took 15 years for someone to break down the psychological wall created by Cunningham's assertion.

As both an athlete and a doctor, Roger Bannister studied and worked to do what no man had done before. Leaders go first and set new standards. Since his breakthrough, over 250 Americans followed his lead. More than 950 men around the world have succeeded in breaking the four-minute barrier.

Clearly, Bannister had determined his direction and goal. The cool thing about his accomplishment, however, is that Bannister shares his triumph with two other runners. When he documented his miracle mile, Bannister wrote that he grabbed Chris Brasher and Chris Chataway and celebrated. They had done it together. The "first" Chris paced Bannister for the first half-mile, the "second" Chris pushed Bannister for the second half. Bannister's dream became a reality because he attracted two partners who followed his initiative, shared his passion, and aimed to meet his standards.

How about Hal Moore? In a recent survey of West Point cadets, the majority identified Lieutenant Colonel Hal Moore as the most inspirational officer in their cadet experience. (You may recognize his name from Mel Gibson's film, *We Were Soldiers*.) Why? Moore left a legacy of raw courage and inspirational leadership. But what made his leadership inspirational? Moore set a standard for his men. He prepared his soldiers to set lofty goals and persist until they achieved them. He drilled them in self-leadership. Moore gave his soldiers direction and revealed to them their ability to persevere.

Lieutenant Colonel Moore also fought alongside his men. Before going to battle at the Ia Drang Valley of North Vietnam, he told his men, "When we go into battle, I will be the first to set foot on the field, and I will be the last to step off. And I will leave no one behind. Dead or alive, we will all come home together." Moore's men didn't fight just because they were part of the U.S. Army. They also fought because they had a Lieutenant Colonel who cared for them, fought with them and set the pace. And you know what? Moore brought every one of his boys home from Vietnam. In fact, throughout his 32-year career, he didn't abandon a single soldier on the battlefield. Moore's skill attracted soldiers, but it was his fatherly example that won their loyalty and sacrifice. Not once did he ask his men to take a risk he wasn't willing to take first.

This was a man who had a compass in his head and a magnet in his heart.

Goethe once wrote, "Look at a man the way that he is, and he only becomes worse. But look at a man as if he were what he could be, and he becomes what he should be." As leaders, it's our job to see potential in the people with whom we work. We must go first and set the standards. But we have to set our standards high. When you challenge your team to reach for high standards, you're asking them to reach their potential. Low standards won't strengthen them. In fact, Goethe would even argue that you're hurting them. Why not be the first to do something? Encourage your team to reach high and dream deep, and together you can take new territory. Perhaps you'll even go where no man has gone before...

REFLECT AND RESPOND

Reflect on some historic or current leaders who "went first." Some may have been hesitant to heed this call, while others immediately embraced the challenge. Let's look at both categories.

Name at least one leader who hesitated to go first. Briefly explain.

_____

_____

_____

What's hard about going first?

_____

_____

_____

Name at least one leader who immediately embraced the challenge. Briefly explain.

_____

_____

_____

What's rewarding about going first?

_____

_____

_____

SELF-ASSESSMENT

Evaluate yourself by responding to the following questions:

1. Am I leading people into new territory? What are we doing that no one has done before?

_____

_____

2. Do I know what kind of standard I am setting for those who are following me? What is it?

_____

_____

3. Am I making them stretch? Or do I allow people to be comfortable and indifferent about growth?

_____

_____

4. What is it that attracts people to my vision?

_____

_____

5. What is it that may discourage people from joining me?

_____

_____

EXERCISE

Invite someone from outside your team or organization to sit in on one of your meetings. Once they are familiar with your goals, ask for their input. From their perspective, what could you change that would revolutionize the way things are done? Get some new ideas. What is a resource or service you could offer that would make you the Roger Bannister of your campus or industry?

Next, sit down with your team and discuss what you could do that no organization has done before. From the list of ideas you have, what is one item you could do to lead the pack? What's never been done—so that if you did it, you'd set an entirely new standard? Once you determine this service or resource, begin laying out plans to pull it off.

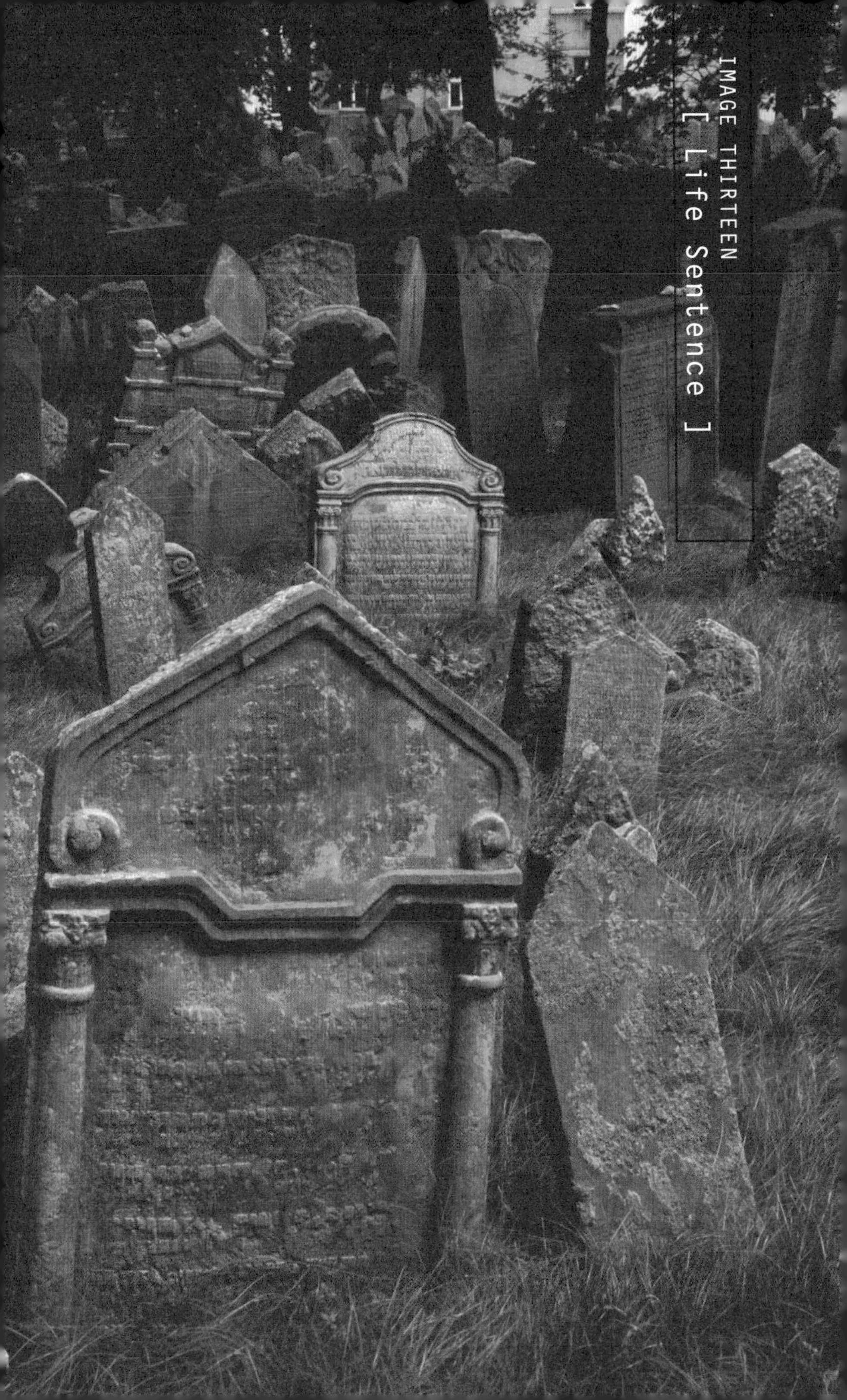

IMAGE THIRTEEN

[Life Sentence]

Life Sentence

THE CONTRIBUTION OF A LEADER WILL ULTIMATELY BE SUMMED UP IN
ONE SENTENCE. ALTHOUGH WE PARTICIPATE IN MANY ACTIVITIES, WE'RE
REMEMBERED FOR JUST ONE OR TWO. WHAT WILL YOUR SENTENCE BE?

This might be the most important *Habitude* of all. That's why I saved it until the
end. It's a *Habitude* not just about how you lead others, but how you lead your life.

For years, Growing Leaders, our non-profit organization, has led students through
experiential leadership programs. One of the exercises is to visit an old graveyard.
We arrive early in the morning or at sunset and instruct the students to walk
through the graveyard and carefully read the tombstones. In these old graveyards,
the stones almost always have an epitaph. We ask our students to reflect on the
person who lies beneath that gravestone... knowing only the information found
in the epitaph. We quickly identify that some died young; some died in old age.
Some were married; some were not. Some attempted to live purposeful lives...
others did not.

After about thirty minutes of gazing at the tombstones, we gather as a group and
discuss what we've read and seen. We talk about those folks who are long gone, and
about our own families, our own dreams and how much time we have left on earth.
Believe it or not, this discussion time is often emotional, as we stop long enough
to think about what really counts in life. Many express regret over how they've let
their lives get so hurried and frazzled. They know they're not living the life they
want to live, nor the life they were meant to live. More than anything, however,
students think about what one sentence might be on their own tombstone. It's
something that will happen to every one of us. George Bernard Shaw once said,
"Death is the ultimate statistic. One out of one will die."

Here's another way to think about it. Years after you die, people will be in a
conversation at the office, on a campus, or maybe at a church. Somebody will
remember you, and bring up your name in conversation. After a pause, someone
else will ask about what you did. The person who responds will likely do so in
one sentence. That's all. They'll describe the entirety of your work and life in one
sentence.

I know you deserve a paragraph. Possibly even a chapter, or a book on what you've accomplished. But, alas, time only permits one sentence in that brief conversation.

Claire Luce Booth first popularized this idea when she observed that ultimately history usually summarizes the contribution of a leader in a single sentence. Who was George Washington? Who was Andrew Johnson? How about Dwight Eisenhower? Each get a headline for what they did. It may not be fair, but it's true.

Here's my question for you. What will your sentence be? I believe you can influence that sentence now by the way you live your life. Are you living your life on purpose, or by accident? Do you know your purpose in life, or do you simply react to life as it comes at you? Do you play offense, or just defense with your life? Are you choosing your sentence?

Thinking about how we want to be remembered is sobering. It is also very telling. Benjamin Franklin, who accomplished so much as an inventor, philosopher and statesman in the early days of America, had this statement prepared for his gravestone: "Benjamin Franklin. A printer. Food for worms."

Reading the epitaphs on tombstones can be enlightening and funny at the same time. Some of the more entertaining epitaphs you can find in graveyards read as follows:

"Sir John Strange. Here lies an honest lawyer, and that is Strange."

In a Thurmont, Maryland cemetery: "Here lies an atheist. All dressed up and nowhere to go."

On Margaret Daniel's grave in Richmond, VA: "She always said her feet were killing her, but nobody believed her."

YOUR SENTENCE

On a more serious note, I believe every one's "life sentence" ought to be unique, based on their personal passion, burdens, values, natural talents, and opportunities.

I am never interested in learning leadership simply for leadership's sake. I want to do more than increase the profits of a company when I lead. I want the world to be a better place because I invested my life in people.

When we choose our life sentence early, we become proactive with our agenda. Life is no longer about merely reacting to the circumstances. In fact, I believe identifying your life sentence opens your eyes to opportunities to fulfill it. I discovered this in 1990, while in New Zealand. I was speaking to students when I became consumed with the deep emotional and spiritual needs of the country. It wasn't that I felt I had all the answers to the problems I was seeing in the students, but I became very alert to the needs and any opportunities I had to address them.

Less than an hour later, I boarded a small, single engine plane to fly to our next site. While trying to land the plane, our pilot got into trouble. The engine stalled, and we dropped 120 feet to the ground. It was a miracle the four of us lived, as we crash-landed on a field. It was a bloody mess but we all survived. The other three men on board were quickly taken to the emergency unit at the hospital. I was escorted to a nearby home to rest. While I was nursing my wounds, there was a knock on the front door of this home. When my host answered it, he discovered news people from the two national TV networks in New Zealand. Evidently, this plane crash was the number one news story of the day.

They asked if anyone was present who saw the plane crash. The host quickly told them he had a guy in the back bedroom who'd been in the plane crash! They asked me if I'd be willing to do an interview. I saw an opportunity coming and said yes. They stood me up, leaned me against a tree in the yard and said, "Tell us what happened."

That sounded like an opportunity to me. I began talking about the miracle of surviving the plan crash and the importance of focusing on what really matters in life—instead of getting caught up in the small stuff. I then spoke about the importance of my relationship with my family and close friends, and my commitment to my life purpose in that critical time. They kept the cameras rolling. In the end, I got to communicate some important truths to three million New Zealanders at the 5:00, 6:00 and 11:00 news that night. It was astonishing.

Question: Would I plan the events to happen that way again? Not a chance. But I have found that by choosing my "life sentence" early in life, it has opened up opportunities to live it out every day, even in the worst of times. My life sentence enables me to live with the end in mind.

REFLECT AND RESPOND

Have you ever tried to summarize your life in a sentence? What would you want to be remembered for in one sentence?

_____

_____

_____

_____

Discussion: If you died today—what would people say was your life sentence?

_____

_____

_____

_____

How does your life reflect your values, beliefs and leadership? Take a moment and evaluate yourself.

1. My lifestyle vividly displays my values and my purpose in life:

< POOR 1   2   3   4   5   6   7   8   9   10 EXCELLENT >

2. I have a clear understanding of my one-sentence purpose in life:

< POOR 1   2   3   4   5   6   7   8   9   10 EXCELLENT >

3. People can tell what my purpose is by the way I lead others:

< POOR 1   2   3   4   5   6   7   8   9   10 EXCELLENT >

4. I am aware of my influence and consider how I affect others in my life:

< POOR 1   2   3   4   5   6   7   8   9   10 EXCELLENT >

EXERCISE

More than one hundred years ago, a Swedish chemist named Alfred Nobel opened up his morning newspaper and got quite a shock. He found his name listed in the obituary column. The columnist had confused him with his brother who had recently passed away. Hmmm. What an interesting predicament. Alfred had the opportunity to read his life sentence in the paper! Here is what he read, "Alfred Nobel, a chemist, died a wealthy man. As the inventor of dynamite, he enabled people to kill each other more efficiently than ever before."

Reading those words was an eye-opening experience for him. He was actually being remembered for inventing dynamite and for aiding the death of multitudes. Clearly, that was not how he wanted to be remembered. So, Alfred took action. He set his wealth aside in a fund that was to be given to people who fostered peace not killing. This fund still exists today and is known as The Nobel Peace Prize. What's more, I love what Alfred Nobel observed late in his life. He said, "I believe everyone deserves a chance to change their obituary in the middle of their life." I agree. And that's what I want to do here.

What is your life sentence? Consider these elements as you attempt to write it out:

1. Your talents?

2. Your burdens?

3. Your passions?

4. Your values?

5. Your acquired skills?

6. Your desires?

7. Your opportunities?

_____
_____
_____
_____
_____
_____
_____
_____
_____
_____
_____
_____
_____
_____
_____
_____
_____
_____
_____
_____
_____
_____
_____
_____
_____

[NOTES]

[NOTES]

Special
Thanks!

"I want to thank a team of people who helped to shape this book, including Margaret Spars, Abbie Smith, and Bethany Elmore. And a very special thanks to Anne Alexander, who proofed and edited the manuscript; and, the Growing Leaders team, who model these principles day in and day out. I love you guys."

Enjoy Habitudes?

Help us bring these lessons to students who can't afford them.

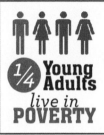

1/4 Young Adults *live in* **POVERTY**

8/10 Young Adults *plan to* **MOVE HOME** *after College*

In both urban and rural environments, **students are sheltered** *within a 9-mile radius of their home,* **shielded from experiences** *that involve risk or failure.* **This leads to delayed maturity.**

All over the country and in developing nations around the world, there are students who are not equipped to lead themselves (or others) into the next steps of their lives. What's worse, their schools can't afford leadership development materials to help them mature into the best versions of themselves.

We want to change that. We want to help students broaden their vision, take bigger risks, think bigger thoughts, and pursue bigger goals.

To do this, we created **The Growing Leaders Foundation**, to provide *Habitudes* in schools and youth non-profit organizations that cannot afford to purchase programs for their students. Thanks to donor support, grants are available for qualified applicants.

To apply or donate, visit
www.TheGrowingLeadersFoundation.com.

The
GROWING LEADERS
Foundation